design your garden with

Linda Ross

SIMON & SCHUSTER
AUSTRALIA

First published in Australia in 2004 by
Simon & Schuster (Australia) Pty Limited
20 Barcoo Street, East Roseville NSW 2069

A Viacom Company
Sydney New York London Toronto

Visit our website at www.simonsaysaustralia.com

Cataloguing-in-Publication data:
Ross, Linda K.
Design your garden.

includes index.
ISBN 0 7318 1139 9.

1. Gardens — Design. 2. Gardening. I. Title.

712.6

Cover and internal design by Caroline Verity Design
Typeset in The Mix and Trade Gothic
Printed in China through Colorcraft Ltd., Hong Kong

10 9 8 7 6 5 4 3 2 1

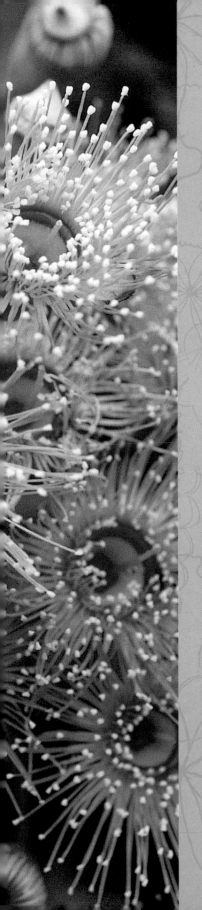

In memory of India Verity

Acknowledgments

My deepest love and respect for my green-blooded parents, Sandra and Graham, who instilled a love of people, family and plants.

Big-hearted thanks to:

My second family, the legendary team of *Ground Force* (series 1 and 2) – Graham 'Big G' Ross, Steve 'Richo' Christianson, Trevor 'TJ' 'Robbo' Robertson, Richard 'Tricky' Creaser, Scotty 'Dugong' Thomson, Lou Cifuentes, Peter 'Pedge' Murray, Timothy 'Britzy' Britz, Pascal Fox, Patrick 'Rico' Thompson, Steve 'Jugga' Jones and Katherine 'Jim' O'Brian and Sarah 'Mother' Adorjany. Who could forget the challenge of designing 38 gardens in 52 weeks — we were driven by naivety, passion and our love of a laugh.

The brave owners of the gardens, who never quite knew what they were going to end up with. I admire your trust.

To all who wake up to me on Saturday mornings on Sydney Radio 2GB. There are 300,000 of you and I thank you for listening. You guys keep me up to date with latest trends and quirky ideas, reassuring me that there are real gardeners out there.

My publisher, Simon & Schuster, particularly my editor, Julia, for her patience on my first book. Caroline, my designer, who helped the words and images dance off the pages.

Gunthe and Geiter Rembel for their garden at Reverie, Dural, which was the inspiration for the Mexican garden.

My girlfriends, Jada, Charlotte, Meredith, Jessica and Tess, who keep me on the straight and narrow, and make my life zing!

Trevor Robertson, who provided emotional support, technical know-how and the inherent ability to say what I always needed to hear.

Oh and Indigo, the greatest blue heeler a girl could have.

Credits: The photograph on page 15 was taken by Phil Aynsley; the map on page 110 was created by Ian Faulkner; and all other photos and sketches are by the author Linda Ross

contents

introduction

For ten million Australians, gardening is their favourite form of relaxation, making it the most popular hobby in Australia. The garden has become an important vehicle for self-expression.

Australians go to great lengths to plan, research, assemble, construct and create outdoor living spaces. A beautiful garden reduces stress, improves relaxation and creates harmony. On top of all this, a good garden increases the property value of our property.

While there are many inspiring books on garden design, they are mostly not Australian, nor do they describe the exciting journey of how you can achieve a beautiful garden for yourself. This book aims to guide you through a simple step-by-step journey, showing you on the way that every garden is unique, responding to a unique group of factors, least of all your own personality.

There are no hard and fast rules when it comes to designing a garden. The garden is a place to express your individual personality and therefore it should remain free from any trends, recent fashions, fads and crazes. By following my step-by-step garden design process, which I have developed over years of designing home gardens, you can quickly and easily design the garden you've always wanted. In the process I will help you tap into your own creativity and unleash it into the garden beyond.

To create the garden of your dreams you need a few basic practical facts. I begin by showing you how to look and assess your land, how to start your own garden design book, collect information, understand the design elements of a garden, and then how to translate ideas from your design book into reality. Look out for the tips on how to make this as easy as possible. And because gardening should never be a chore, I include hints on how to make it pleasurable. Important practical information on topics such as types of soil, watering, fertilising, mulching, potting and pruning, plus suggestions on saving time, effort and money are also included.

This is a practical garden guide to gardening with soul. To inspire you I reveal five of my best garden designs. Each garden displays a unique design, terrific planting ideas, plant profiles, simple creative projects and practical garden advice. Use them, abuse them, stretch them, contort them or shrink them. Borrow from my experience to create your own living masterpiece.

The aim is to inspire and encourage you to place your personal imprint on the design of your garden. Some of the plants I suggest may be inappropriate for your location, in which case look around your neighbourhood to find plants that fulfil the same objectives as the ones I have recommended. The best way to discover what grows well in your area is to go for a walk, take pictures, make friends with the best gardener in the street, and chat up the local nursery person — they have a wealth of information.

So don't waste any more time, **start now.** With my help, you can create a beautiful garden beyond belief. **Happy gardening!**

think

Gardens are soul places. Design your garden to reflect your personality, individual style and flair. Use the garden as your canvas and start painting now. Be as bold or as restrained as you like. It's up to you ... express yourself!

Designing your own garden is one of the most enjoyable and rewarding domestic tasks because it involves all parts of the brain. You'll need a bold vision and the foresight to make it work. Throughout the design process you will have to make careful, rational decisions while letting yourself go wild with the design. Don't be daunted by such elements as light, shade, energy and space. These are exciting and challenging factors that are unique to garden design.

In the following pages I will show you the best way to approach your garden makeover by using my easy step-by-step guide. I will guide you through the process while alerting you to the pitfalls and reminding you of the facts. I will take you through all the stages of designing your own garden, whether you have a pocket-sized courtyard or a typical suburban block.

ABOVE: *Don't be afraid to make an impact with design tools such as scale, perspective and proportion.*

ABOVE: *Revel in the tiny intricacies of the natural world.* BELOW: *Be inspired by the natural lines of the larger landscape.*

getting started

CREATING A GARDEN
WITH A SPIRIT OF PLACE

To me my garden is an extension of my soul and an expression of my personality. To others it may look rough around the edges, but my garden brings me peace, serenity and enormous pleasure. I wander through it daily noting new arrivals: little shoots, fruits and flowers. My year is linked to seasonal surprises — the glowing green shoots of spring, the tracery of wintry willow branches, the first ripe tomatoes of summer. Without a garden I occasionally think I would be nothing — I would be completely ill at ease with the world, with nowhere to hide and indulge my creativity. My garden has nooks and crannies, places to entertain, places to hide and a place to grow organic vegetables for the family. It delights all children who visit, and provides me with constant wonder, pleasure and work.

Aspire to create your own distinct garden. A place where you can feel comfortable and at peace with your surroundings — somewhere to spend your leisure time and enrich your life. A garden can empower your inner spirit and restore your energy. In a garden you are away from the responsibilities and structure of the world outside, far away from the hustle and bustle, phone calls and emails. It is somewhere that transports you further into yourself and provides you with the vast satisfaction that all is well, happy and at peace in your immediate world.

When starting to plan your garden, think about what kind of place you wish to live in. Is it bold, quiet, formal, or chaotic and exciting? You are creating your place. One solitary idea alone can achieve a spirit of place. A place is quite different from a space. Your place should combine your personality, mood and atmosphere and entwines your character to allow for meaning and attachment.

PLANNING

Start the planning stage by listing what you wish to achieve and how you will go about realising these goals. Begin the process by gathering as much information as possible so you can make informed decisions. Look through books and magazines, browse the Internet, go to garden open days. Discover various ways of doing things, such as landscaping techniques, and find interesting new materials so you can accumulate a palette of ideas on which you can base important decisions. Good planning will reduce the possibility of costly mistakes! And forget what you've heard, planning can be fun.

First, you need to thoroughly understand the climate of your site. In particular, note all the opportunities it offers and the constraints. Try and turn what you perceive to be constraints into positives, go with it rather than against it. For example if you have a windy block, design a garden with tough sculptural wind tolerant plants. If you have a damp dark site, plant a rainforest. If you have sandstone floaters and shallow soil, don't go formal, go with an Australian bush garden planted in the pockets. Working with what you have makes things much easier and the long-term results will be more successful.

The more information you collect about your property the wiser your choices will be and ultimately the more enjoyment you will get from your garden. Before you begin designing, it is best that you live in the house and monitor the changes in the garden,

ABOVE: *Here are some tools of the trade. Buy pens in a range of thicknesses and colours.*

such as patterns of sun and shade, over one year. This may sound extensive and tedious but it will ultimately cut down on silly mistakes. Every property has a number of different microclimates, such as a suntrap on the western side, shade on the south side and usually sun all day in a garden that faces north. Knowing these types of details will lead to better plant choice and overall garden success.

garden sketchbook

Buy a large sketchbook to use as your garden sketchbook. A garden book is my favourite tool in the garden design process; it records your progress and is the place to keep all your snippets, thoughts, ideas, cut outs, paint colours, materials and plant names safe. Within its pages you can write down all your aspirations, desires, loves, dislikes, dreams and thoughts about your garden.

Buy a sketchbook with lots of pages. Your garden sketchbook will become the brain of your garden. It will double as an encyclopaedia and diary of events. Later, you will enjoy looking back through it to see how your garden was conceived.

---

tools of the trade

When designing your garden you will need the following:

- pens and pencils
- grid paper
- blank & tracing papers
- scale rule
- long tape measure
- eraser
- camera
- circle templates
- property plans that may have come with the purchase of the house
- service plans (water, electricity, sewer)
- ring the Waterboard for water and sewerage plans
- ring your local council for property plans
- ring 'Dial before You Dig' for the location of underground services

---

In your garden sketchbook, begin by:

1. Listing what you want from the garden.
2. Collecting garden images that appeal to you.
3. Listing the advantages of the property.
4. Listing the disadvantages of the property.

LIST YOUR DESIRES

Every person is unique and so it follows that every garden will be different too. A garden can have various forms and functions. In your garden book, list what you want to do in your future garden. The more you want from your garden, the more complicated the design process will be. So plan your garden to suit your needs. Ask yourself who the garden is for.

Gardens come in all shapes and sizes, and in all styles. Your garden will need to address many issues and satisfy a long list of demands. List them in your garden book and refer to the list when you draw up your final plan. They may include:

- ▶ **A sunny timber deck** close to the house and kitchen to entertain friends and family.
- ▶ **Hard-wearing lawn** for children and dogs to play on, visible from the house.
- ▶ **A water feature** to provide a frog refuge.
- ▶ **Plants** to provide colour intensity, flowers and interest all year long.
- ▶ **An arbour with a deciduous climber** on the western side to provide relief from summer sun.
- ▶ **A peaceful nook** that must be serene and tucked away – a good spot for some morning yoga!
- ▶ **A hedge** for privacy.
- ▶ **Ornaments** throughout the garden to add your own personal touch.
- ▶ **Irrigation and mulching** to keep the hard work down.
- ▶ **An outdoor barbecue area.**
- ▶ **Garden furniture**, including an outdoor table setting.
- ▶ **A hidden hammock** for you.

photographs

Photographs are the best way to view the existing three-dimensional shapes of your garden. They are also a practical recording device and helpful in discovering effective solutions.

You can draw your ideas over the top of them on tracing paper to help you find the right scale and proportion. Refer from the photographs to the ground plan and be aware that the plan provides only a bird's-eye view. Not all gardens look good in plan — a plan is a tool, not the final destination.

COLLECT GARDEN IMAGES THAT APPEAL TO YOU

Now is the time to begin collecting samples of materials that will contribute towards the look you're striving for in your garden. Collect anything that takes your fancy. Hardware stores, specialist landscaping suppliers, junkyards, garden centres, fabric shops, antique shops and auctioneers all have wild and interesting samples. Recycling depots have fascinating wares, such as containers, glass bottles, industrial items, used railway sleepers and slate roof tiles. Take photos, collect samples, cut out pictures and clippings from magazines, and glue everything into your garden book. Soon a panorama of possibilities will appear before your eyes.

ABOVE: *I collect ideas for my subtropical garden. Pictures of pots, paints and plants torn from magazines go straight into my garden sketchbook.*

ABOVE: *I like the fact that there is an existing wisteria and that the back garden has dappled shade.*

LIST THE OPPORTUNITIES OF THE PROPERTY

Take time to list in your garden book what you see as your property's opportunities. Every property will have positive aspects that provide the perfect conditions to create a stylish garden for entertaining friends or to meet your need for privacy. In my garden I found the following to be positive aspects that I could really work with:

▶ **Large area**, empty canvas.
▶ **Dappled sunlight** on back lawn, perfect for summer.
▶ **Good deep soil**.
▶ **Pleasant views** to surrounding gum trees that create a forest feel.
▶ **Nice sunny aspect** to read morning newspaper over breakfast.
▶ **Gentle slope** that aids drainage.
▶ **Back deck is the perfect height** to see over and into the garden beyond, making a great viewing platform.

LIST THE CONSTRAINTS OF THE PROPERTY

Conversely every site will usually have some constraints, or negative aspects that will need to be addressed and their dilemmas solved from the word go. They might be simple things like an ugly shed that can be easily removed, or they could be more difficult, like having very little sun. It is essential to appraise the garden in this critical way. A successful garden is one that takes everything into consideration. This following list was the negative aspects that I listed initially for my property.

▶ **Little privacy on eastern boundary**, but good open views that make the garden appear larger.
▶ **Large Norfolk Island pine** in back garden takes up a lot of moisture from the soil.
▶ **Very little sun in winter**, problem for drying clothes.
▶ **Open to the westerly sun**, which makes house hot in summer.
▶ **No privacy in front garden**.
▶ **No pathway around the garden** to walk through the garden.
▶ **No access from back deck** to garden.

ABOVE: *I worry about the existing Norfolk Island pine sucking up too much moisture. On the other hand, it gives the garden a heart and scale.*

LIST POTENTIAL SOLUTIONS

Good garden design starts with problem solving and moves onto creating mood and impact. Start by thinking of a range of solutions. For example if we were to take the above list of constraints, I see the following solutions. These solutions become the basis of your initial garden design.

- Need an **interesting flowering hedge** on eastern side of property with gaps in the hedge to glimpse into the garden beyond.
- **Plant bromeliads** and other epiphytes that don't have roots under the large Norfolk Island pine.
- **Remove 10% of the canopy of overhead trees** to allow more sun in. Check first with local council and if the trees are large, like my enormous blue gums, get in an experienced tree lopper or arborist
- **Use a deciduous tree** on western side to create summer shade and allow in the winter sun.
- Start thinking about a **thick privacy hedge** along front boundary.
- Need an **informal path** that matches with the forest feel so as to take visitors on a tour around the garden.
- **Build a new set of wide stairs** from the back deck straight into the garden.

ABOVE: *Bromeliads are the solution for me. They love dappled shade and they don't need soil to grow.*

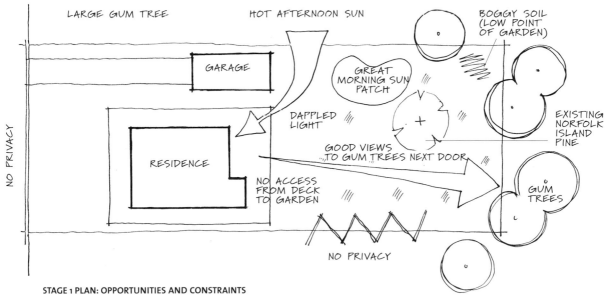

STAGE 1 PLAN: OPPORTUNITIES AND CONSTRAINTS
Write the opportunities and constraints down over a sketch plan of the garden.

13

inspire
tropical

Come outside. Enjoy! Enclose yourself in the colours of summer. Paint the garden in lipstick pink. Spice it up. Drink in the flavours of cardamom, ginger and lemongrass. Sweet, sour, pungent. It's time to apply some heat.

Tropical gardens are found across the globe, in places like Thailand, Bali, Hawaii, China, Fiji, Australia and Brazil. Each region has its own feel, symbolism and plant material. In general the tropical garden is bold, dramatic, colourful and slightly chaotic, filled with symbolism, tradition and meaning. The frangipani is often planted in these gardens as a traditional offering, while the sacred lotus is prized as the symbol of perfection. The tropical garden is full of strong culinary flavours and based on a simple design where colourful foliages predominate. Tropical Chinese gardens rely on orchids and bamboos to create lush and colourful gardens. Flowers and perfume are essential — scents such as frangipani, moonflower and cardamom create a further dimension.

taste of the tropics

GARDEN DESIGN PLAN

Tropical gardens rely on drama, colour and intensity. The simplicity of the curvilinear design contrasts with the chaotic 'jungle' nature of the planting. The main grassy area curves around to terminate at the focal point — a thatched pavilion. Luscious palms, colourful foliage, rattan furniture, bamboo torches and brightly coloured pillows complete the picture. Remember the addition of perfume, which goes hand in hand with a tropical garden. The deck is the perfect place to view the riot of colour and see the floral tops of the frangipanis.

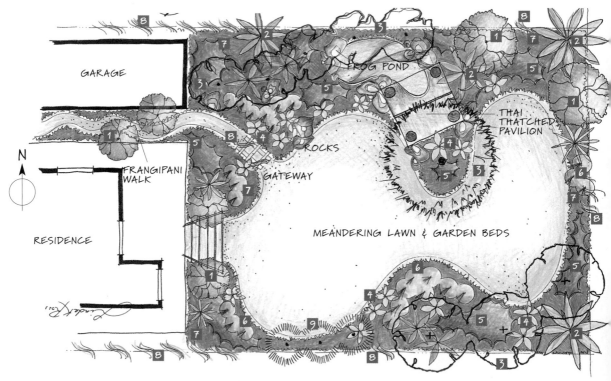

PLANTING KEY
1. Frangipani
2. Banana, Lady Palm, Tree Fern
3. Birds Nest Fern, Cycad
4. Buckinghamia Lemon Myrtle Blueberry Ash
5. Cordylines, Ginger, Crotons, Canna Lily
6. Ixora chinensis
7. Bromeliads, Sedum
8. Tropical climbers
9. Chinese Lantern, Vireya tropical Rhodos

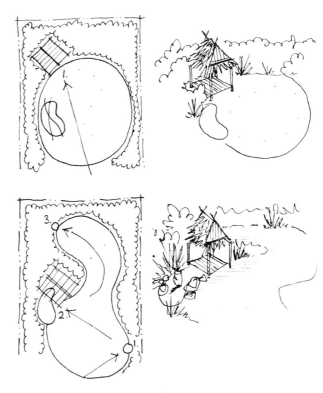

SUITABLE CLIMATES

Tropical and subtropical zones. It is near impossible to create a tropical garden in cooler areas of Australia. A true tropical garden should never experience frost or temperatures below zero.

DESIGN TRICKS

By bringing the Thai hut in towards the centre a little, we make a hidden area beyond. This creates intrigue and another 'secret' place.

By incorporating the pond into the garden near the Thai hut we have integrated the elements and created a more synchronistic approach. A protected pond is safer for birds and frogs as it offers more shelter from predators.

The meandering lawn offers opportunities for us to personalise our garden with sculptures. Don't overdo it, the rule is to allow the viewer to see parts of only one or two sculptures at a time. Having them partially hidden increases the element of surprise, which leads to greater enjoyment.

PLANTING SCHEME

Gardening in tropical and subtropical areas requires a different approach from cool climate gardening. Tropical gardens rarely have to be dug. Just layer the soil with composts, leaf mould, garden clippings and mulches. Leaf mulch layering is a natural process in forests and gullies where soil fertility resides in just the top few inches. The other significant feature of gardening in the tropics is the need for a good pair of secateurs. Anyone who gardens in warm, high rainfall climates knows that during wet periods plants seem to burst out of the ground, usually over everything else. They must be pruned into submission or they will go rampant.

The taste of the tropics is easy to emulate. Planting schemes are based on an explosion of flamboyant foliages and perfume. Most tropical

OPPOSITE: *Large garden beds filled with colourful foliages curve to enclose the garden space. A bold design balances the dramatic foliages and forms.*
ABOVE: *Play around with the position of garden elements to create interesting niches. Build anticipation and discovery by manipulating and creating spaces.*
BELOW: *In Bali, the frog is a symbol of happiness.*

gardens rely on foliage rather than flowers for interest. Foliage should be fresh, lively and colourful. Planting in groups of odd numbers — three, five, seven and nine — is a common trick of the trade of garden designers to give a broad brushstroke of colour and texture. This will make a huge difference to the entire feel of the garden. Place contrasting foliages next to each other to create drama and interest. Here is our list of bright, bold, and colourful plants to give year-round colour and interest to a tropical garden.

GO TROPPO WITH FRAGRANCE

Surround yourself with fragrant frangipani for those hot balmy nights. Tropical orchids can perch on tree trunks for spring sweetness. Swathes of cardamom release perfume after rain, while the pure white scented blooms of the gardenia give the eye a well needed rest.

tropical climbers

Plant moon flower (*Ipomoea alba*) near an outdoor entertaining area so at dusk you can watch the pure white flowers open as big as saucers and surround you with their delicious fragrance. Bougainvilleas, mandevilla and the golden trumpet vine (Allamanda cathartica) are all glorious climbers for a tropical garden. Use climbers to mellow vertical surfaces and cascade over walls, fences, sheds and arbours. Try this selection of fast and furious climbers to give you the impact you need quickly.

- Chinese star jasmine
  (*Trachelospermum jasminoides*)
- Madagascar jasmine (*Stephanotis floribunda*)
- Brazilian jasmine (*Mandevillea* hybrids)
- Rangoon creeper (*Quisqualis indica*)
- Golden trumpet vine (*Pyrostegia venusta*)
- Jade vine (*Strongylogon macrobotrys*)
- Queen's wreath (*Petred volubilis*)

planting list

- Abyssinian banana (*Musa mannii*)
- Angel's trumpet (*Brugsmania* spp.)
- Bamburanta (*Ctenanthe oppenheimiana*)
- Bat plant (*Tacca integrifolia*)
- Bird's nest fern (*Asplenium spp*)
- Black bamboo (*Phyllostachys nigra*)
- Brazilian orchid (*Oncidium varicosum*)
- Bromeliad (*Vriesia, Guzmania, Aechmea*)
- Canna lily (*Canna* 'Tropicanna', C. 'Tricolour')
- Cordyline (*Cordyline* hybrids 'Wik's Gold', 'Lemon Lime', 'Morning Sunshine')
- Heliconia (*Heliconia rostrata* 'Crab's Claw' *Heliconia angusta* 'Yellow Holiday', 'Hot Rio Nights', 'Red Xmas' , 'Sexy Pink')
- Crotons (*Codiaeum variegatum*)
- Elephant's ears (*Alocasia x amazonica*)
- Fijian fire plant (*Acalypha wilkesiana*)
- Hibiscus (*Hibiscus rosa-sinensis*)
- Japanese sago palm (*Cycas revolute*)
- New Guinea impatiens (*Impatiens*, New Guinea hybrids)
- Ornamental ginger (*Alpinia, Globba, Curcuma*)
- Poinciana (*Delonix regia*)
- Prayer plant (*Maranta leuconeura* 'Kerchoviana')
- Sedum 'Gold Mound'
- Soft tree fern (*Dicksonia antartica*)
- Spider lily (*Crinum pedunculatum*)
- Spiral ginger (*Costus* spp.)
- Tropical rhododendron (Rhododendron, *Vireya* cultivars)
- Zebra plant (*Calathea zebrina*)

TROPICAL FRUITS

Feijoa, babaco, breadfruit, guava, passionfruit, mango, pawpaw, miracle fruit, sapote, tamarillo, starfruit, avocado, mangosteen, pineapple, custard apple.

Heleconia 'Sexy pink'

Bird's nest fern

Crab's claw

Shell ginger

Cordylines love dappled shade

Fishtail Heliconia

plant profiles

 height & width of plant

 good for pot

 prefers full sun

 prefers partial shade

 tolerates full shade

 frost hardy

 frost tender

BELOW: *Torch ginger emerges from the ground and comes in red, pink and white.*

ORNAMENTAL FLOWERING GINGER

Alpinia, Curcuma, Zingiber, Costus
Globba, Etlinger, Hedychium

    1 m–4 m

bold foliage, unusual flowers

Ornamental flowering gingers grow quickly to give a lush, exotic and tropical feel to your garden. The edible ginger is just one of hundreds of beautiful gingers available for the home garden. Grow away from direct sunlight and shelter them under the canopy of taller plants. They require protection from strong sun and winds. Gingers are herbaceous perennials that die back after flowering; the plant is usually dormant over winter until new shoots emerge in spring. The exotic flowers of the ornamental gingers come in a variety of shapes and colours, providing a long lasting display for up to ten weeks..

> Rich fertile soil and a warm moist atmosphere will encourage good growth. Keep ornamental gingers in a sheltered position and protect them from frost and full sun.

One of the hardiest gingers, *Hedychium flavens* can grow nearly anywhere but most of the other gingers (*Curcuma, Alpinia, Zingiber, Globba*) need tropical to subtropical conditions. Many of the gingers used in this garden come from the forests of Asia and the Pacific. Look out for these varieties:

▶ *Curcuma alismatifolia* 'Siam Tulip'
▶ *C. cordata* 'Jewel of Thailand'
▶ *C. rubescens* 'Ruby'
▶ *Zingiber parishii* 'Lemon Lights'
▶ Beehive ginger (*Z. spectabilis*)
▶ *Globba winitii* 'Thai Beauty'
▶ Red ginger (*Alpinia purpurata*)
▶ Red torch ginger (*Etlinger elatior*)
▶ Spiral ginger (*Costus* spp.)
▶ Edible ginger (*Zingiber officinale*)

LADY PALM
Rhapis excelsa

   4 m x 1 m

multi-trunked with pleated leaves

The lady palm is a multi-stemmed palm from southern China that forms sensational clumps. These palms look great bunched together or as a stunning single specimen. Preferring a little protection from full sun, the lady palm can be grown anywhere. Raphis can be kept in pots indoors, remaining in the same pot for years without the need for repotting. Keep the moisture up in summer and propagate by dividing the plants into half. Palms such as this and the ones listed below create the middle and upper canopy of the tropical garden.

Leave the Cocos palm behind in the last millennium and be inspired by other beauties. There are so many exciting palms to choose from that exhibit a large range of foliage shapes and textures. Try the fan palm if you desire huge round leaves circling the sky, or the brilliant red stems of the lipstick palm. Perhaps you'd prefer the shining silver fronds of *Bismarkia* to provide a deliberate foliage contrast. Golden cane palms are great for adding privacy. Even bangalow palms look good when planted together in a grove. Some palm varieties grow up to 10 m tall, so it is always wise to check the label before planting one.

Palms can be expensive to buy, so consider planting them from seeds or tube stock. They will establish more quickly and their root systems will be stronger than if you plant mature specimens.

- Alexandra palm (*Archontophoenix alexandrae*)
- Bangalow palm (*Archontophoenix cunninghamiana*)
- *Bismarkia nobilis*
- Cabbage palm (*Livistona australis*)
- Fan palm (*Licuala ramsayi*)
- Golden cane palm (*Chrysalidocarpus lutescens*)
- Lipstick palm (*Cyrtostachys renda*)

Look out for the rare silver Joey palm (*Johannesteijsmannia magnifica*), a magnificent giant with curious pleated leaves spanning over a metre in width, with striking silver colour on the underside.

FROM LEFT TO RIGHT: *Beehive ginger flowers; 'Jewel of Thailand' ginger; Lady palm.*

> Palms grow quickly in the tropics, often shooting up in five years. In the south, they can take longer, often taking up to ten years to reach full height.

plant profiles

FRANGIPANI

Plumeria rubra hybrids

  5 m x 4 m, perfumed flowers

the flower of the Pacific

BROMELIADS

Vriesea, Guzmania, Neoregelia

    0.4 m x 3 m

excellent foliage colours

The thick, fleshy stems propagate easily from cuttings in early spring. Be wary of the poisonous milky white sap. Ensure success by letting cuttings dry out for 7 to 10 days before planting. Keep frangipanis well mulched.

There is nothing like the sweet fragrance of frangipani on a balmy summer evening. No tropical garden should be without one or two! These delightful umbrella-shaped trees bear masses of perfumed flowers in summer. Colours range from pure white, cream with golden centres to salmon pink and carmine red. The flowers are best viewed from above or as a floral carpet after they fall. Deciduous in winter, their fleshy branches provide interesting winter tracery. If you find the bare stems unattractive, plant hibiscus or any of the plants listed here to disguise the trunks.

Create your own jungle floor ecosystem by using an old decaying log and some epiphytic bromeliads. Drill holes into the log and glue the bromeliads into place with builder's adhesive. Remember that bromeliads are epiphytic, which means they receive their nutrients through their leaves not the roots and soil.

Bromeliads quickly grow into huge colourful clumps. Being epiphytes, bromeliads don't need soil. Their unusual shapes and kaleidoscope of colourful foliage light up dull, lifeless shady areas. Their leaves form a central moisture trap, reducing the need for frequent watering. In their natural habitat, frogs lay eggs in each well as the tadpoles are assured of a safe and nurturing environment.

FROM LEFT TO RIGHT: *Fragrant frangipani; A costus with delicious flowers that can be added to salads; A bromeliad flower spike which lasts for up to six months; The long flowering blooms of an ixora flower.*

Bromeliads love growing in inexpensive pine bark chip. The bark allows the bromeliad to drain freely and easily. Don't use normal soil or potting mix, as it will hold too much moisture and cause the plant to rot. Broms are great for growing en masse under large trees with large root systems.

In humid conditions bromeliads can grow anywhere, even on tree trunks — just ensure their central well is kept full of water. Increase their number by removing the side 'pups' and transplanting them into bark chip when they reach 10 cm long.

Remember bromeliads only flower once, so it is important to cultivate new 'pups' so you can enjoy continuous flowering. Flower spikes often last up to six months. When the flower spike eventually dies back, remove it right at the base. And take this as a warning: Bromeliads are addictive.

JUNGLE FLAME, *IXORA*
Ixora chinensis 'Prince of Orange'

   1.2 m x 1.2 m

showy fiery flowers

This small tropical shrub bears spherical clusters of tangerine rocket flowers that resemble shooting stars. Cloaked in glossy evergreen foliage, it provides a wonderful low backdrop to other foliage accents.

Ixora needs a warm, frost-free environment with high humidity in order to flower throughout the warmer months. Keep well mulched and feed with compost or leaf mould. Recent cultivars include 'Splash', a yellow-flowering variegated form which is not cold tolerant. 'Kampon's Pride' is a white-flowering cultivar.

> *Ixora* are susceptible to root fungus, so ensure the soil is mounded and drains well. They need a warm, frost-free, partly shaded position with rich soil. Prune after flowering has finished in order to keep the plant compact.

design features

EDIBLE HERBS AND SPICES

Grow a variety of edible Asian herbs and spices in your tropical garden. Cardamom, kaffir lime, lemon grass, coriander and mint grow well among other tropical shrubs in shaded, moist spots. Edible ginger (*Zingiber officinale*) should be planted in September — just plant a healthy looking green ginger rhizome bought from the grocer. It will be ready to harvest in March or April. To harvest, dig up each clump with a spade. Not only do Asian herbs and spices provide wonderful flavours for cooking, they have a fantastic aroma and deter insects from the garden.

ginger drink for colds and flu

Ginger is a wonderful spice used to reduce symptoms of cold and flu. This traditional Russian recipe came from an old neighbour when I was a child, we've used it ever since. It is a superb concoction to prevent flu and sore throats.

- *2 x 1 cm cubes of fresh ginger root sliced fresh from the garden*
- *2 small cloves of garlic, crushed*
- *2 teaspoons honey*
- *1/2 teaspoon ground paprika*
- *juice of one lemon or lime*

Fill cup to top with boiling water. Leave for 3 minutes to infuse. Strain and drink.

FOCAL POINT

This Thai hut is a retreat from the hustle and bustle of everyday life and is the central focal point in the tropical jungle garden. Here one can sit, relax with friends or read the morning paper in total privacy. The thatched pavilion adds a unique architectural element. The high-angled roof is thatched with brush to blend in with the jungle theme. The large feature turpentine posts were recycled from an old wharf. Their rough bark adds a more natural effect than dressed timber posts.

Use tea-tree brush as a cheaper alternative to prefabricated thatch roofing material. Second-hand brush will give an aged shaggy look to your pavilion, giving the impression it's been there for years.

FROG POND

Hidden away, surrounded by bromeliads and feature rocks, this pond makes the perfect home for frogs and lizards. Be wary of the material you use to construct your pond if you want to encourage wildlife, as most metals will be toxic to frogs and fish. If you use concrete, remember to leave it for a few days to cure before adding fish. Tropical water lilies need five hours of sunlight a day. Choose native fish like mountain minnows — they won't eat the tadpoles but will keep the mosquito larvae at bay. Place a stainless steel grid just below the water surface to keep the water feature safe for children.

GARDEN CARE

Tropical gardens are simple to maintain; it's a matter of clip, tidy and feed. Trim off any brown or dying foliage, trim flowers once they are finished and mulch thickly with fallen leaves. Feed your garden with a mulch of well rotted organic manures every spring. Spray all the foliage with a seaweed solution once every season to keep the plants robust and healthy.

Most gingers die down in winter so remove all the shaggy, dying foliage. When the weather warms up, feed with aged manures as soon as the new foliage appears. They will need regular moisture during their growing season.

Bromeliads will constantly surprise you with their hardiness and vigour. They flower only once and then bear new plants from the side called 'pups'. Cut

the pup cleanly away with a sharp knife when it reaches about 10 cm. I like to let them clump naturally. Bromeliads don't have to be planted in the garden, they can be attached with an old stocking to tree trunks or even to the posts of the Thai hut.

CREATING A TROPICAL STYLE GARDEN IN COOLER CLIMATES

If you live in a cooler climate and are dying for a tropical look, try this range of hardy tropical-looking plants: bird of paradise, New Zealand flax, cordylines, canna lily, hibiscus and bangalow palm. The bright tropical colours of orange and pink can be achieved with plants like New Guinea impatiens, petunias and groundcover verbena. Hide your fences with colourful climbers such as bougainvillea. Gingers will be most successful planted in a warm sheltered spot near a north-facing wall. Keep well mulched over winter with thick pea or garden straw. If frost causes them to die back wait for warmer weather, as they will usually grow back from the base. Choose heady varieties of ginger, such as hedychiums and alpinia for these cooler zones.

the potted water garden
Seal and fill a glazed pot or half wine barrel with rainwater. Submerge a waterlily for an elegant and sculptural form. Sit the pot on bricks so the leaves are the right level. Choose from hardy and tropical waterlilies, depending on where you live. The flower is absolute perfection, comes in pure white, lemon yellow, pink, blues and purple. Feed each spring by placing a water lily fertiliser tablet 10 cm into the soil. You can add other water plants such as sweet flag, Japanese iris and *Cyperus papyrus* for a vertical element to the living water arrangement.

BEFORE

plan

Time is on your side. Sit back and watch for a while. Take a long deep breath and ask: Where does the sun rise? Where does the water settle? Don't rush. Don't skip the page. The section 'Think' is where we start to think things through, now we start to plan. Accuracy is the key, so let's get it right the first time.

The aspects unique to your block will gradually inform the design of your garden. Start by collecting site-specific information, such as climate, drainage, boundaries, views and microclimates. This information is best collected in layers. Each layer can be overlaid to create the complete picture.

ABOVE: *Don't overlay any old design over your garden. Each garden should respond to its own unique set of site-specific factors. This garden took its lead from the existing banana and jungle feel.*

start with a site plan

Use grid paper for your site plan to help with accuracy. A scale ruler will come in handy but if you prefer, you can simply use a normal ruler. In which case mark each centimetre as one metre (1:100). To make it easier, you may need to enlarge your plan on a photocopier later.

STEP ONE: THE PROPERTY BOUNDARY

The original property survey makes a great starting point. You usually receive this at the time of buying the property. If you do not have one, you can make your own. Begin by noting the boundary dimensions and accurately locating the house within the property. Be precise by marking off each house corner point from two boundaries. Put all these measurements down onto paper and transfer your site plan to grid paper. At a later stage you will be using these measurements to estimate sizes, amounts and costs, so get them right now.

Add the entrances and windows to the house outline like the plan shown here. This will help with the alignment of pathways and to set up certain views from inside. Add the location of the driveway and garage if you have one.

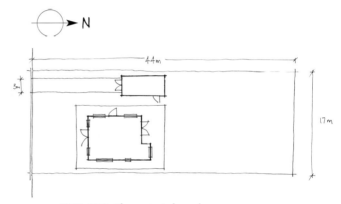

STEP ONE: *The property boundary*

STEP TWO: THE SITE SURVEY

Locate all existing features on your property. Accurately position each of the features on your grid paper by measuring with a long tape measure the distances from the two closest boundaries. Mark the present clothesline, all existing plants including trees, shrubs, groundcovers and hedges, any outdoor living area, rocks, barbecue and garden shed. Mark all these measurements on the grid paper. Note any special features that you see, like the neighbour's specimen tree. Take a measurement of the size and width of tree and shrub canopies.

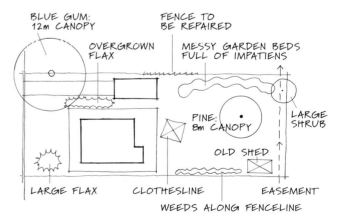

STEP TWO: *The site survey*

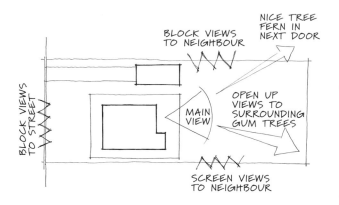

STEP THREE: *Photograph main views*

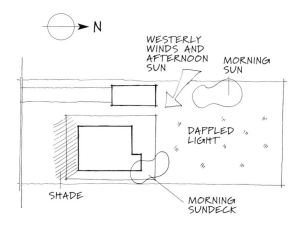

STEP FOUR: *Climate*

STEP THREE: PHOTOGRAPH MAIN VIEWS

Note the main views from the windows within your home, and from different positions in your garden. Decide whether you want to borrow anything from the surrounding landscape. Think about each view as having a foreground, middle ground and background. Your neighbour may have a beautiful feature tree you want to incorporate in your garden design. Panoramic photographs are an excellent tool for taking in sweeping views and recording the information to provide you with a point of reference. This is also a good time to check if and where you need to add privacy.

STEP FOUR: CLIMATE

Mark a north point on your plan. Note the direction the sun travels across your garden, then mark the sunny and shady spots, heat traps and the direction of the prevailing wind. Be aware that the patterns of sunlight and shade change from winter to summer as the sun becomes higher in the sky. Observe your garden, as you will have several different sets of growing conditions that will need different approaches. The main areas of sunlight and shade will quickly become apparent, but you might find a few areas that are shadier in the cooler months.

This house faces south, which means the front garden is shady while the back garden gets sunshine all day as the sun crosses from east to west. An easterly facing block will get morning sun, while a western aspect usually gets a blast of afternoon heat. The direction a garden faces affects not only the plants that can be grown successfully but also the placement of garden features, such as ponds, clotheslines and outdoor dining areas.

Frost is one limiting factor in any garden. Depending on where you live this could be a serious issue. During winter record the number of frosts and where they occur on a copy of the site plan. This will impact on your plant selection later on. Some areas of the garden might be frost free, like areas around the house or in protected spots, mark these areas too. Snow and cold winds are also limiting factors.

STEP FIVE: SOIL

This is the time to check what sort of soil you have. Does your soil crumble or make clods? Is it made up of coarse sand particles or finer clay ones? If you're worried, take a sample into your local nursery for assessment. If you are really motivated, test the pH with a home testing kit. This determines the acidity or alkalinity of the soil. I've never worried about this as it only becomes important when you are growing pH sensitive plants like rhododendrons, pieris and kalmia, all of which thrive in lime-free acidic soils and mountainous conditions. Good soil needs air pockets and nutrients, for more information on improving your soil see page 111.

STEP SIX: DRAINAGE

During periods of heavy rain observe where the water flows across your property. Watch for any pooling water or channels after rainfall. You may need to add extra drainage. Drainage is essential and it is best solved sooner rather than later. Any boggy, wet areas and areas of pooling water indicate inadequate drainage. Good drainage can be achieved with a variety of different systems depending on the amount and location of the water, and the function of that area.

Few gardens are level. The high and low points of the property will give you an idea of where the ground water flows. With a naturally sloping block, rainwater will run down, across the contours. Make sure no water runs towards or along the foundations of the house. If the block is fairly flat with only a slight slope, you can do the drainage yourself. If it slopes steeply, it is wise to get an expert in. Drainage is the first thing to install and get right. It's amazing how the hidden things are often the most important.

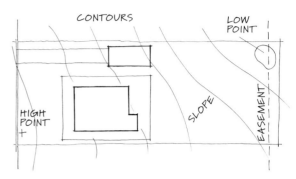

STEP SIX: *Drainage*

drainage

TRENCH DRAIN

This is a system of trenches laid in a grid pattern under the surface of your lawn, gardens and paving areas. They work using gravity. Constructed on a slight gradient they are filled with gravel. Lengths of agricultural pipe are laid in the trench, wrapped in geotextile material to filter the soil and sand particles out of the water helping the flow.

ABSORPTION PIT

This is a large pit filled with gravel into which water seeps. This should be located far from built structures and is best for friable and sandy soils.

DRAINAGE GRILL

A catchment grill or drainage holes are used in paving to collect surface water and connect to the storm water. Paving should always be laid on a slight gradient to help carry pooling water away.

Congratulations! You have now completed the site plan of your property. Make a few copies of the plan and glue one into your garden book. Now it's time to move beyond the initial site 'plan' into further garden planning. It's time for revision, assessment and thoughts about long-term maintenance and budget.

practicalities

DECISION TIME

Unless you have a bare block, there will be some existing features that will need to go. This is the time when you have to be brave and make decisions. Assess what you want to discard and what you want to keep. Plants that are in the wrong spot will need to be moved or just plain thrown out (oh, I mean mulched and put back into the soil). On one copy of your site plan, discard everything you would like to see removed by going over the lines with liquid paper. This will give you a clean, fresh start. If something doesn't fit into your overall scheme, get rid of it. Remember to get council approval to remove any large trees or you could be up for a hefty fine. Glue another copy of the plan into your garden book and make a few corrected copies for the next stage.

MAINTENANCE

When planning your garden, it's important to think about how much time and effort you are willing to put into your garden. Let's be practical ... it's no use planning a garden that needs constant effort. Busy people with busy lives don't have a lot of time to garden. Think about how many hours a week you are able to spend working in the garden, and whether it would be wise to reduce the garden areas or simplify the planting. Consider the type of materials and surface areas within the garden, such as lawn, gravel areas and paving. Lawn and grass require more maintenance than paved areas.

There are many ways of reducing maintenance in the garden. A friend of mine with an incredible garden swears he spends no more than four hours a year maintaining it. Here are the top six rules for a maintenance free garden.

- ▶ Reduce lawn areas to a minimum.
- ▶ Plant evergreen trees rather than deciduous.
- ▶ Plant tough plants like succulents and bromeliads.
- ▶ Install a micro irrigation system on a timer.
- ▶ Plant slow-growing hedges.
- ▶ Resist planting bulbs or annuals.

UTILITIES

Don't forget the essentials. It is easy to get caught up in the design without considering the practicalities, such as a place for the garden hose, the lawnmower and the clothesline. They will all have to fit somewhere. Some essentials to remember are:

- ▶ A garden shed to store bikes, outdoor toys, equipment and garden tools.
- ▶ Car parking spaces plus the garage or carport.
- ▶ A lawn area for pets and children to play.
- ▶ Paths, paving and clothesline.
- ▶ A place to hide the garbage bins.
- ▶ An area for the compost bin or heap.

REVIEW

Review your desires and your solutions. For each desire cut out a paper bubble that is to scale and label it, for example, 'pond', 'privacy hedge', 'barbecue', 'outdoor living area'. Place the bubbles over your corrected site plan and move them around, overlapping them. Each bubble indicates a desirable function and has nothing to do with design. The purpose of the bubbles is to locate each desire and notice how it interacts with its neighbours. Ask yourself specific questions. Where would you want to sit, relax, entertain, picnic or play? Is it a sunny spot? Is the compost too close to the entertaining area? Is the shed in the right place? What will happen if that tree comes out? Does the vegetable garden get enough sun? Can you fit all your bubbles into the garden? If not, which ones can be sacrificed?

Don't forget to provide somewhere to store your growing collection of garden materials and tools.

When you're happy with the placement of the bubbles, glue them onto the site plan and place a copy into your garden book.

BUDGET

At some point you will start thinking about how much all this will cost. Try not to let your budget restrict your creativity; in fact some of the most inspiring and awesome gardens I have seen were created on a shoestring budget. Of course the reverse is also true, but gardening on a shoestring can be fun. Take up the challenge!

12 ways to save money in your garden

1. Go to auctions, recyclers and second-hand shops.

2. Salvage unwanted bigger plants from building sites and older gardens to help make your garden look more established. Frangipani, camellias, grasses and old roses are all easy to move. This is best done in autumn or winter when the plant is dormant.

3. Get plant cuttings from friends and neighbours in late summer and propagate them. Simply dip the end of a 10-cm cutting into root hormone powder and plant five cuttings into a pot. Leave the pot in a semi-shaded position and water regularly. By autumn the cuttings will have developed good root structure and can be planted out into the garden in early spring.

4. Plant from seed where possible.

5. Make your own compost and soil improver with fallen leaves and kitchen scraps.

6. Collect stable manure to add to your soil to improve its organic nutrient level.

7. Establish a worm farm. You can then gather free liquid fertiliser that can be collected, diluted and watered on to the garden.

8. Grow a lawn from seed or runners rather than buying turf in rolls.

9. Look up second-hand building material companies in the Yellow Pages. Look out for ones that sell second bricks, pavers and pots.

10. Make your own focal points, sculpture and interesting water features with found items or reused industrial pieces. Your local tip is a great resource, as well as curb-side clean-up days. It's amazing what people throw out.

11. Look out for mail-order nurseries. Not only do they stock interesting and unusual collections but offer bulk-purchase discounts. Shopping can now be done from the comfort of your own home or with the ease of the Internet. This reduces the threat of the dreaded 'impulse' buy. See the list of my favourite mail-order nurseries in the appendix.

12. Buy in bulk. If you need lots of compost to establish a garden and can get hold of a trailer, buy a trailer load. It is much cheaper than buying by the bag.

inspire

mexican

Not for the faint-hearted. Desert landscapes alive with the blazing sun, blue skies and golden barrels lined with lethal spines. Hints of colour against a sepia earth. Playful sounds from running rills of cooling water. Fresh. Fun.

Hot days, water restrictions, drying winds and drought make 'no water' gardening an exciting alternative. With smart plant choice and preparation, you can have a garden inspired by the desert gardens of Mexico and Santa Fe. Dry desert gardens combine tactile textures, interesting materials and colours. The sounds of crunching gravel underfoot, the desert look of adobe, wood, large terracotta pots and bright Mexican colours combine to create a great garden style. Light, free-draining sandy soil is better than dark nutritious soils, as these desert plants have adapted to poorer soils. Be inspired by this simple design and sensational plant combinations.

mexican dry garden

GARDEN DESIGN PLAN

An Aztec or Mexican-inspired garden is a dramatic and highly artistic environment. Handmade arts and crafts, hand-painted artworks and your own sculptures will all fit into this theme. Striking and simple dry gardens have a lot to offer.

This garden revolves around a cool bubbling centre. This provides a cooling magnet on hot summer days. To capture the desert sensation, the surrounding concrete block walls are bagged to achieve an adobe finish and a sun-bleached look.

Deco-granite and white quartz give the ground interest and texture. Towering cactus contrast with sweeps of soft grasses. A rill transports cool running water into the centre of the garden and deposits it into a circular pond. The water flow quickly cools the hot dry courtyard.

Pathways converge around the bubbling cool heart. Paths lead from one place to another, taking you on a magical journey of discovery, delivering you to a desert planet alive with striking triffid-like plantings and deep shadows.

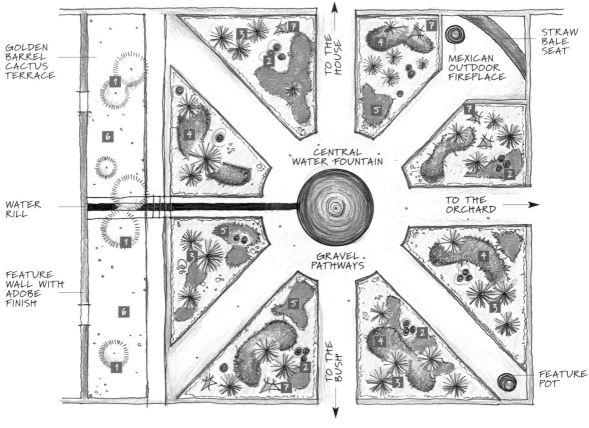

GOLDEN BARREL CACTUS TERRACE

WATER RILL

FEATURE WALL WITH ADOBE FINISH

TO THE HOUSE

CENTRAL WATER FOUNTAIN

GRAVEL PATHWAYS

TO THE BUSH

STRAW BALE SEAT

MEXICAN OUTDOOR FIREPLACE

TO THE ORCHARD

FEATURE POT

PLANTING KEY
1. Golden Barrel Cactus
2. Mother-in-law's Tongue
3. Tall Cactus
4. Pride of Madeira & Ornamental Grasses
5. Succulents
6. Pebbles & Rocks
7. Century Plant

ABOVE: *Triffid-like plantings push the limits of the imagination. Striking monster shadows move noiselessly across the gravel pathways,*
RIGHT: *A simple circular design contrasts with the complexity of the plant textures, flowers and forms.*

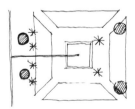

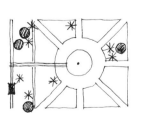

CLIMATE

Arid, cool and temperate zones

PLANTING SCHEME

Bright colours accentuate the muted tones of drought-tolerant plants. Drama and impact is created with bold forms of New Zealand flax and other grasses. Contrasting textures and forms achieve a sense of visual excitement and drama. The sweeps of soft grasses blowing in the breeze bring movement

into the garden. They are in stark contrast to the spines and prickles of the cactus. Sculptural swathes of succulents, planted in large groups, create a patchwork effect. Succulents propagate readily from leaf so obtaining large numbers is an easy task. Cacti and succulents give incredible structure and backbone of the garden, while naturalistic plantings of softer perennials blur the boundaries.

planting list

- *Aeonium arboreum* 'Zwartkop'
- Arctotis hybrids 'Apricot', 'Flame'
- Blue chalksticks (*Senecio serpens*)
- Blue fescue (*Festuca glauca*)
- Californian lilac (*Ceanthothus* sp.)
- Century plant (*Agave attenuata*)
- *Cotelydon orbiculata*
- Day lilies (*Hemerocallis cultivars*)
- *Echeveria elegans*
- Flanders poppy (*Papaver rhoeas*)
- Golden barrel cactus (*Echinocactus grusonii*)
- Golden sedum (*Sedum adolphii*)
- Lavender (*Lavandula* hybrids)
- Miscanthus (*Miscanthus sinensis* 'Strictus')
- Mother-in-law's tongue (*Sansevieria trifasciata*)
- New Zealand flax (*Phormium tenax* cultivars)
- Pride of Madeira (*Echium fastuosum*)
- Rock rose (*Cistus x hybridus*)
- South African daisy (*Osteospermum ecklonis*)

Take your shoes off. Sit down. Cool off.

Running water cools the surrounding air and adds a playful element to a formal courtyard. Fountains, pools, spouts and rills of running water create 'white noise' and a lively atmosphere. Water provides a dramatic contrast to the almost austere planting combinations.

Echeveria elegans

Arctotis

New Zealand flax

Century plant

Flanders poppy

plant profiles

 size & shape of plant

 good for pot

 prefers full sun

 prefers partial shade

 tolerates full shade

 frost hardy

 frost tender

LEFT: *Mother-in-law's tongue.* **RIGHT:** *Golden barrel cactus.*

MOTHER-IN-LAW'S TONGUE
Sansevieria trifasciata 'Laurentii'

    1 m x 0.4 m

vertical leaves patterned with yellow

Grow mother-in-law's tongue in sandy soil as it dislikes being kept moist. Can be grown indoors in a well-lit room.

Resilient and sculptural, this plant provides an excellent vertical element in a garden or pot. The dark green leaves are banded with yellow and cream and have a quirky twist as they grow. Superbly tough it will withstand complete neglect, great for a bachelor pad.

GOLDEN BARREL CACTUS
Echinocactus grusonii

    1 m x 1 m

perfectly spherical form

The golden barrel cactus is a perfectly spherical barrel that stores liquid in its swollen stem. The stem can swell to as much as one metre wide and weigh a tonne. Golden yellow spines protrude like barbs in a radial pattern. This tough and some-times savage cactus bears a ring of pretty, delicate, yellow flowers at its crown in summer. Keep it away from pathways and mass plant it in a group for the best effect. For something a little smaller, try *E. pasacana*, which is small enough to fit on a sunny windowsill. Water from the base and fertilise in spring. Clump two or three together for the best effect.

When moving spiky cactus around the garden, protect yourself by first wrapping the cactus in bubble wrap. The bubble wrap will stop the spines from touching and penetrating the skin.
Wear heavy gloves as well, you can't be too careful with cacti!

FROM LEFT TO RIGHT: *Variegated agave with Flanders poppies. Pride of Madeira and an aptly named pink form, tower of jewels.*

AGAVE

Agave species (A. americana marginata)

    1m x 1m

brilliant accent plant

> Feed cacti with a controlled fertiliser twice a year and remember to give them a good soak occasionally during their growing season.

Loved for its bold form and striking variegated leaves, this is the perfect accent plant. The leaf margin is defined by a line of sharp barbs, so plant within garden beds away from busy areas such as pathways and children's play areas. Accentuate the contrasting form by combining with softer plants, grassy foliages and pretty flowers. Agaves need well drained soil and warm conditions.

PRIDE OF MADEIRA

Echium fastuosum

    2 m x 3 m

iridescent purple flower spires

This large sprawling shrub bears a halo of indigo flower spires in spring. Its silver grey leaves are soft to the touch. The intense flower display makes it an ideal companion to lavender, daisies, succulents and grasses, plus it performs well with very little fuss.

> Cut echium back hard at the end of the flowering period. The pieces will propagate easily from 10 cm cuttings when struck in a sandy mixture. Its tolerance of salt-laden winds makes this large shrub great for coastal areas. Look out for its sister *E. wildpretii*, which has an elegant, single coral pink flower reaching up to two metres tall.

plant profiles

LEFT: *Cereus.* **TOP RIGHT** *Aeonium 'Sunburst'.* **BOTTOM RIGHT** *Aeonium arboreum 'Zwartkop'.*

PERUVIAN TORCH CACTUS
Cereus uruguayanus syn. C. peruvianus

     4 m x 0.5 m

tall cactus, great shadows

Cereus store their moisture in their fleshy stems. They aim straight for the sky and create dramatic vertical lines in the landscape. Feed in spring and mulch well. They will delight you with their white waterlily-like flowers at night during summer. Cereus are best when grown unrestricted so they are able to fill out into a wide clump.

> Look out for the utterly delightful electric blue *Pilosocereus seupremus*. This sensational tall cactus is best grown in a sheltered protected position, in full sun, away from harsh winds. Or keep it inside as a pretty pet.

AEONIUM ARBOREUM 'ZWARTKOP'
Syn A. 'Swartzkoff'

    0.6 m x 0.5 m

striking purple/black foliage colour

This sensational succulent, with its striking black leaves that resemble huge floral rosettes, comes from Morocco. Rosettes are held on long stems, creating a bold display of colour and form. The plants prefer full sun but grow well in partial shade. Aeoniums produce true flowers occasionally, and when they do they are a real treat. Yellow clusters of flowers billow brightly from the plant.

> Prune flowers back when finished. These plants make terrific potted sculptures. Look out for a variegated form with gold and cream leaves called 'Sunburst'.

design features

FOCAL POINT

The innovative straw bale wall will not only add an authentic feel to your Mexican garden but will also be a practical feature. Built of straw and rendered with cement, this durable wall fits perfectly in a dry desert garden. Mark out the location, dig a footing trench and fill with concrete. Insert reinforcing bars vertically into the footing while still wet. When dry, paint the footing with a waterproofing agent. Impale bales of compressed double packed straw onto the reinforcing bars and lay them in a stretcher bond pattern for extra strength. Cover the bales tightly with chicken wire. Trowel 20 mm of cement render coloured with oxide over the chicken wire. We have chosen an ochre-sandy colour. When the first layer is dry, finish with another 20-mm layer of coloured oxide cement.

GARDEN CARE

Water cacti at the base and not on the growing points. Allow to completely drain after watering. Water fortnightly throughout the growing season and stop entirely during the winter months. This way they will stay strong and vigorous.

Most cacti have little use for nitrogen-based fer-

tiliser as these encourage soft growth that is prone to rot. Use a controlled-release fertiliser throughout the growing season — spring and summer — to supply essential nutrients. This fertiliser lasts up to six months. Propagate by removing lower leaves and striking them in cactus mix. Keep succulents and cactus in plenty of sunlight and preferably in raised beds or pots.

Trim back grasses to ground level at the end of winter with a whipper snipper to allow new growth to come up from the base.

ABOVE: *A favourite of mine from Mexico,* **Agave victoriae-reginae,** *is a fabulous living sculpture all of its own.*

the potted desert garden

Try transforming bland pots into exciting Mexican-inspired designs with tile mosaics. Use brightly coloured ceramic tiles to give your old pots a lift. Simply glue the pieces on to the pot with tile adhesive, wait 24 hours and then grout. Colourful cacti, succulents and bright trailing verbena look great in these colourful pots. Their shallow root systems make these plants perfect for pots which can be used to liven up a rooftop garden.

construct

Dip into this collection of fabulous features. Designing your garden needs creative drive. Don't be frightened by the idea of 'creative', just sit back and absorb the features from this chapter. Take them, change them and make them your own. Push the boundaries, construct your vision and most of all, have fun!

Now that you have completed the site plan you will have already considered most of the planning issues. This chapter takes you through the garden elements and components you may wish to use in your garden design. The first section of the chapter explores the framework and structures within your garden. Look at the entrance and boundaries, and the best spot for outdoor living. Design your pathways so people can weave through and experience the garden from all angles.

The second section explores focal points and features. Place water features and sculpture, in strategic positions to attract the eye and lure you onwards. This is where you can add those special touches that make the garden really yours — decide on the style of garden ornament you want to include.

Finally in the third section, we discuss how to choose your plants.

Choosing one type of style does not mean it will be there forever — a garden will change and evolve over time. Colours, moods and meanings change and then become a memory. As your lifestyle changes, so too will your garden. Choose a style that speaks to the architecture of the house and has a dialogue with the interior. Look at the transition zone between the house and garden. To blend the outside with the inside, construct a pergola or deck. Moderate your style with a touch of reality and ask yourself the tough questions: Are you intending to sell the property later? Are you planning any additions in the future that might impact on the garden?

OPPOSITE: *Don't be a gardener who never rests. Plan a spot to place a bench where you can relax. Dress it up.*

creating a framework

Each garden is made up of different elements, so planning a garden is like making your own living, breathing jigsaw. A dynamic garden is built upon a strong framework and interesting softening effects. The purpose here is to understand all the pieces of the puzzle.

First create the framework by deciding on the built elements. Then move to surfaces and then to the softer more organic and seasonal influences, like plant material. Some of our favourite garden elements, such as water features, walls, fences and ornaments, are included in this chapter. The elements at your disposal can be mixed and matched depending on your style and ultimate vision.

A cohesive garden design will be achieved when you have a good understanding of the materials available to you and how to use them. Many materials that you thought could never be used together can and interesting effects. can be acheived by mixing and matching. Wonderful finishes can be created by placing materials with contrasting textures and colours together. When you find a material you like, take a sample or photo and add it to your garden book next to other materials and ideas to see if they visually work together. Remember to take the name of the supplier, note specifications and the cost.

I love hunting to find interesting and unusual materials as they contribute to truly unique gardens. If you have the time, try your luck at junkyards and recycling places — you never know what you'll find. You know the drill: someone's junk is someone else's treasure. The most interesting pathway I have seen was made out of the bottoms of glass bottles set into a concrete. The bottles were green and blue and glistened like aquamarine in the dappled sunlight, a watery path with moods that changed with the cloud reflections.

ABOVE: *Make an entrance. See what a difference it makes to arriving home.*

YOUR GARDEN ENTRANCE

Every good garden, like every good socialite, needs a grand entrance. What can be more satisfying than arriving at your own home. An interesting entrance increases the anticipation of what lies beyond. The idea of coming home from a tiring day at work, finally opening your gate into your private world beyond makes you all the more eager to leave work. Whether it's a homemade gate made of driftwood or a carved Balinese double door, an entrance says more about you and your garden than you may realise. Choose the style of your gate carefully as it will inform the character of your house and garden.

OUTDOOR LIVING SPACES

Outdoor living areas are important fresh, bright living spaces. Planning an outdoor living room is like planning a room inside, you need to take sun and wind into consideration and decide how they link up to other areas. They can be simple — a place to sip your coffee and read the paper. They can be secret — a hidden hammock to get away from it all. Or they can be elaborate — places for lunching the day away with friends. Party places are important areas in the garden, especially with Australia's perfect climate; there's nothing better than your own private party zone. You don't need a large space or a big budget to enjoy your own backyard retreat.

Start by picking the right spot. This will result in the perfect stage for memorable social events at all times of the year. An area close to the house and kitchen is a good choice for frequently used spots. Maybe a level area that connects to the house and takes in the view of the entire garden A level spot will be more functional. A timber deck is perfect for this. If it is a secret retreat you want, find somewhere tucked away in the trees. Consider a sunny spot, as you'll be able to entertain guests there all year round. If you choose a sunny location, include some sun protection for the summer months. Shade can be achieved with temporary structures, such as umbrellas and fabric sails. Or you can increase the use of your outdoor areas by providing shelter from rain and wind. Polycarbonate sheeting and laser light roofing products will keep you dry while letting in the light. Refer to your site plan for the direction and strength of prevailing winds to decide whether you need to factor in a windbreak.

Children grow with the garden and the nature of their play will change over time as they grow. When they are little, all they need is somewhere soft underfoot with a bit of dappled shade. After a few years the garden will have to meet such demands as space for inflatable pools, swings, hide-and-seek

TOP: *Build child-friendly play areas and your garden will become a hub of activity.*
ABOVE & RIGHT: *Family gardens evolve from simple child friendly spaces to more elaborate entertaining places over time.*
BELOW: *Never forget the garden is a child's first paradise. You have the power to make it an adventure.*

spots and cubby houses, then soccer nets and basketball rings. A large grassed area will come in handy no matter what type of play your children choose. When planning where it should go, think about its proximity to the house, surrounding shade and visibility from the house.

GARDEN JOURNEY

Pathways come in many shapes and sizes. What pathway will suit your garden? How will you move through and around the garden? A straight, flat path will take you where you want to go quickly and result in seeing the garden at one glance. Conversely, a winding path takes longer but can lead to more surprises as it snakes around the garden. Mark the lines on your plan and look at how to integrate and simplify the lines of movement across the garden. Don't change the direction of a path for no reason — if you need a direct route, like the back door to the herb garden, a straight path is best.

One of the most important things about a garden is how one moves through it. An interesting path entices the visitor to start a journey. A garden journey is an ideal way to unwind after a busy day and a pleasant way to share your garden with friends and family. It is amazing how the alignment of a pathway can result in significant changes in the appearance of a garden and how one experiences it.

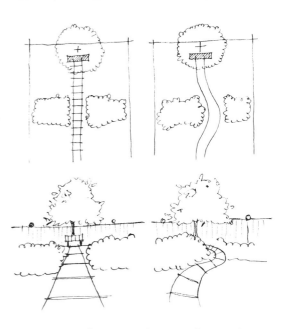

ABOVE: *Seeing the entire garden in one glance can be boring, so curve a pathway to add a little mystery.*
LEFT: *A strong diagonal path provides a functional track. Great for getting to the door quickly.*

LEFT: *Steps and retaining walls create different garden spaces.* **RIGHT:** *Sleek rendered walls suit contemporary courtyards.*

GARDEN BOUNDARIES

Garden walls define the physical boundaries of your garden and create privacy and security. They also provide shelter, create suntraps and reduce wind. Unify the garden with the house by choosing walls that blend with the materials used in the home. There is a huge range of traditional and modern materials available. Think about windows through your garden walls. Windows through walls entice you through to other garden rooms as well as cheering up a blank wall. Garden boundaries come in many forms, built like a wall or fence, or living like a hedge.

Built walls

Be wary with the placement of built walls, they are hard to move once completed. Check with your local council for the regulations that are in place which will influence the height, material and style of wall. An interesting and inexpensive alternative is a straw bale wall. They are surprisingly long lasting. Most walls will need to be built by registered builders and tradesmen.

Living walls

A living wall encloses the garden with soft green barriers and screens of foliage. A short low hedge can also enclose chaotic flowerbeds. If you don't have a great deal of time to spend on trimming, select an informal hedge which is easy to look after and provides a soft garden barrier. Hedges ebb and flow with the seasons, providing year-round interest to your garden. They come in all sorts of varieties — deciduous,

CLOCKWISE FROM TOP LEFT: *Low hedges and formally clipped spheres give pattern and framework to the garden.* ▶ *Pleached hedges should be left to the enthusiast.* ▶ *Have fun with a formal clipped hedge to create a playful garden room.* ▶ *Picket fences add charm to a romantic cottage garden.* ▶ *A reed fence makes a delicious dark background to any garden.* ▶ *Bamboo suits an oriental-style or tropical garden.* ▶ *Post-and-rail fencing is perfect for wide open spaces.* ▶ *Timber slat fences are easy to build, beautiful and certainly won't blow the budget.*

flowering, uniform, mixed, neat, shaggy and edible. Choose the right hedge to match your garden design. Leafy hedges look good all year and should be trimmed in late winter and late summer. Try box, viburnum, lilly pilly and lophomyrtus. Flowering hedges need a little more care. Try murraya, oleander, hibiscus, magnolia, ixora, ivory curl tree and camellia. The rule here is to prune just after flowering. Feed flowering hedges a complete food a little but often.

> *Cut down on time and effort. The fastest and most effective tool is a power hedge trimmer.*

Fences

Fences are useful vertical surfaces that enclose your garden. The sort of fence you choose should directly relate to the style and materials used in the home. An ugly fence can be obscured with a quick-growing climber, while an ornamental fence, such as bamboo or reed, can become a feature in itself. Steel cable fences look great on decks and balconies in beach gardens. Be careful about building brush fences, they are a fire hazard in bushfire-prone suburbs.

SURFACES

Surfaces determine. how your garden functions. Your choice of material will have a huge impact on the feel and look of the final result. Choose from soft, hard, recycled and mixed surfaces to create the look you want.

Soft surfaces

Soft surfaces are essential for pets, families and children. The type of soft surface you want will depend on the overall plan plus the amount of sun and shade the area receives. Meadow grass with mown paths is a romantic alternative to a lawn. Lawns can be established from scratch by seed or with rolls of turf. Remember that a lawn will need constant attention and can be a drain on time and resources, but the positive benefits usually outweigh the constraints. If you're struggling with achieving a

BELOW: *This backyard is a 21st century garden room.*

Try before you buy
Paving costs money, so it's important to thoroughly research the materials, methods of laying and the position of the paved area in the garden. Before construction, lay out the paving in the proposed position, then try out the area with tables and chairs. How does it feel? Is it the right size? Will it be big enough for a large party of friends and still feel right with just one friend? Consider the views to the rest of the garden. Check out the reverse view and see how the area will look from other parts of the garden.

'perfect' lawn maybe it's time to lower your expectations and be happy with a 'Heinz' variety — a bit of everything. At least it will be green and soft underfoot. Be wary of using pebbles in your garden if you have a young family, visiting children or large trees overhead. Pebbles are impossible to keep neat and tidy as overhead trees constantly drop leaves. It has been my experience that kids love to throw pebbles (and take them home with them!).

Hard surfaces

Paved surfaces will make the garden more usable and easy to move around in and enjoy. Hard paving is the best choice for outdoor entertaining areas and heavy pedestrian traffic areas. You can choose from the large range of materials listed below. Scale is important, use smaller paving units to create a larger illusion of space. Restrict the types of materials to a few, and even less for smaller gardens. The combination of too many different materials can end up looking confusing and messy.

Choose materials on the basis of availability and the effect you're after in combination with the surrounding house materials and maintenance requirements. Some surfaces need extra attention, such as reconstituted sandstone that must be cleaned with hydrochloric acid, while real sandstone and bricks just need a spray with a high-pressure waterhose. Light-coloured paving under large trees will quickly be discoloured by tannin from fallen leaves. Types of stone vary depending on the region. Most hard-surface paving you can do yourself if you are methodical, if not, employ a paving expert to get it right the first time. There is nothing more unsightly than sinking or uneven paving.

> Check whether your local paving supplier sells seconds. Some of the imperfections are so small they can't be seen when in place, or if so will become part of the weathering process of the material anyway. You can save up to half of the cost.

- ▶ **Timber decking** wears well, great for entertaining and gives a natural look.
- ▶ **Poured concrete** is the cheapest solution and looks better softened with grassy checkered borders.
- ▶ **Crazy paving** is the most informal way to use stone.
- ▶ **Reconstituted stone paving** squares are cost effective and hard wearing, and look good when designed with decorative patterns.
- ▶ **Slate and granite stone squares** are ideal for formal pathways.
- ▶ **Cobblestones** look lovely and give the cottage character and charm.
- ▶ **Stepping-stones** must be stepped out first before installation.
- ▶ **Brick paving** can come in any pattern you desire.
- ▶ **Bluestone paving** is darker, so it retains the heat.
- ▶ **Terracotta tiles** work well around pools and in courtyards, and are good for transition areas between the house and garden.

BELOW: *Rustic timber sleepers give character and charm.*

CLOCKWISE FROM TOP LEFT:
Different sized pebbles and river boulders create a natural looking creek bed. ▶ *Gravel paths crunch under foot.* ▶ *Repeat pebbles in pots and on the ground.* ▶ *Crazy sandstone paving is rustic and rural.* ▶ *Inexpensive concrete squares can be dressed up by allowing a checkerboard of grass to soften the effect.* ▶ *Formal paths for formal gardens.* ▶ *Green grass is restful and cooling providing functional play spaces for children and pets.*

CLOCKWISE FROM TOP LEFT: *This mirrored pathway reflects the sky above.* ▶ *Pebble mosaics can be colourful and dramatic.* ▶ *Interesting ground patterns formed from stone and brick.* ▶ *Smashed slate is reused from discarded billard tables.* ▶ *The pathways here are made from crushed recycled bricks.* ▶ *Smooth river stones massage the soles of your feet.*

Reused and mixed surfaces

Recycling is hip, reusing is cool. Where possible, look out for recycled materials as they have a weathered look, which creates instant character. Recycled products and materials are advertised in newspapers, local papers and the *Trading Post*; and are available from local junkyards and even some council garbage tips. You can expect to pay much less for second-hand items, plus you'll be helping the environment by reducing landfill — excellent! One design element to consider is mixing different surfaces to provide interesting ground patterns. Placing different materials next to each other will result in wonderful textures and patterns. It is easy to be creative and unique by designing your own paving patterns. Create areas for gravel and stones sandwiched between pavers or sleepers and they are more likely to stay put.

focal points and features

GARDEN BUILDINGS

Garden structures create instant focal points. Pick a style that suits the architecture of your home and garden. A simple terracotta urn in a cottage garden quickly draws the eye. You can place your structure in full view and draw attention to it immediately or you can tuck it away as a surprise. Built structures, such as a Moroccan pavilion, add a further dimension and use for your garden. They become wonderful places to entertain and enjoy while giving you the delight of eating outdoors and experiencing the seasons. One such pavilion I know has been the stage for wild Arabian night dinner parties. By dressing it up with beautiful flowing fabrics, iron candelabras, a low rectangular table and soft colourful cushions, an evocative mood and exotic atmosphere was created.

Use your plan to position the main focal points in your garden, including garden buildings, water features and structures. You may not be able to fit everything in. Remember to plan the views from different points in your garden and to think about how to build things as you go. Now is the time to use those photographs we took in our Plan stage. My tip is to make enlarged black and white photocopies of the photos — this won't cost much. We don't need colour as we're just trying to get the framework of the garden sorted first. Place tracing paper over the photocopies and pencil over any new elements you are thinking about including in your garden. You don't have to be neat — rub out, change and allow the sketches to evolve.

Garden buildings entice us into our gardens. They are places for entertaining and the perfect spot from which to view your creation. Practically speaking, they allow you to store garden tools and equipment. They can also provide shelter and sanctuary.

ABOVE: *Position a garden building to attract mystery, intrigue and attention.* **BELOW:** *Take cover from grey skies and entertain friends in your outdoor garden room.*

The Thai hut shown on this page was chosen for its tropical feel and the laid back nature of the owners. The hut is partially obscured and softened by foliage to entice the visitor within. By positioning the hut in the middle of the garden and planting around it, we gave the garden the added dimension of a secret space. You can use these tricks in any sized property — just enlarge or reduce the scale and proportion to suit your space.

WATER FEATURES

Water is wonderful in a garden, adding lively movement, sparkle and evocative sounds — perfect for cooling down the air. With soaring summer temperatures, a water feature remains the cheapest and easiest way to keep your garden cool and is directly responsible for lowering temperatures.

TOP LEFT: *The traditional summerhouse is versatile, multifunctional and great for rainy days.* **TOP RIGHT:** *A gatehouse is a classic way of adding a formal garden room.* **ABOVE:** *A beach hut continues this garden's marine theme and is a neat way to store garden tools .*

CLOCKWISE FROM TOP LEFT: *A simple water spout powered by a solar panel.* ▶ *Elaborate waterfalls make sensational focal points, adding ambience and movement.* ▶ *This is just one of the ancient water spouts of the walk of 100 fountains in Villa D'Este outside Rome.* ▶ *Modern, fun and well crafted.* ▶ *Turn on the tap to cool the air with this recirculating wall tap.*

Water features have become the catchcry for modern gardens, while in fact they originated centuries ago and have been used ever since. Every television garden has one. They remain the best way to drown out city noises while encouraging wildlife into the garden and creating a mood of serenity and calmness within a small space.

Whether you choose still or flowing water for your water feature, ensure it is well constructed, safe and clean. A broken water feature will quickly become an ugly and mouldy sore point. Check that the construction is sound, the materials used are good quality and the system is entirely waterproof. Use a good quality pump and liner that won't break down in the sun. If you're thinking about adding a simple bubbling water feature, look out for a solar water pump, which can be easily fitted to a water bowl or decorative pot.

CLOCKWISE FROM TOP LEFT: *Even I could knock up this rustic timber gate.* ▸ *Anyone for a quiet game of Pooh sticks?* ▸ *Wrought iron is ornate and inviting. And what a pretty shadow it throws.* ▸ *This elegant timber screen permits intriguing views from one garden area to another* ▸ *A simple seat entices the visitor to stay a while and enjoy. A garden without a seat is like a bedroom without a bed.* ▸ *This geometric framework provides a bold pattern* ▸ *This rustic timber arbor supports boughs of blossoming roses giving dappled shade and a cooling pathway below*

ARBORS, ARCHES, PERGOLAS, BRIDGES AND GATES

Create shade and style in your garden with overhead structures, such as arbors, arches and pergolas. These frameworks are light architectural elements that help the house to fit snugly into the garden environment. Pergolas lure us, tempting us under them to enjoy their dappled shade and shelter. They play an important role in the garden journey — they may lead to another part of the garden or finish at a surprise feature, such as a sculpture, topiary or pond. Consider softening garden structures with climbing plants, which will bring their own perfume, colour and dappled shade.

Other built structures, for example screens and arches, will give your garden a strong framework. Their positioning is also important. Use your garden book for drawing the intended structure over the photographs to help you get the proportion and scale just right. Remember to keep it simple and restrained — don't overcrowd your area with too many structures. One well-designed structure is usually enough.

SCULPTURE AND ORNAMENT

Ornamentation gives your garden personality and character, and expresses its essential spirit. Ornamentation in the garden comes in just about any form you can think of — farm machinery, an old wheelbarrow, carved timber, found items, such as a piece of driftwood or even a smooth stone, have associated personality and history, adding to the overall character of the garden. Whether you choose an individual formal sculpture, make one yourself from found items, or fill your garden with small and meaningful items, your choice will reflect your personality and create an instant bond with your environment. I like to bring these ideas inside creating a link between garden and home.

Sculpture will give your garden a personal and unique touch while adding another layer of interest. Use sculpture to provide a quick focal point, to spice up a drab corner or to create atmosphere. Alternatively, sculpture can finish off a vista or surprise the visitor along the way. Sculpture can be bold, funny, stylish, antique, quirky, shocking and temporary. In the garden designs included in this book I used a range of sculptures to fit in with the owners of each home. Stone brolga birds dancing in the cottage garden create fun and laughter, carved stone frogs for the tropical garden symbolise happiness, an Aztec motif in the dry garden arouses a feeling of spiritual mystery.

BELOW: *Unleash your creative side. Use found and industrial materials to add a quirky touch.*

CLOCKWISE FROM TOP LEFT: *Have you heard of pigs flying?* ▸ *Imported lanterns quickly dress up a Balinese garden.* ▸ *A mirrored obelisk serves two purposes, reflecting parts of the garden and adding a strong focal point.* ▸ *Timber furniture must be protected with linseed solution to keep it impervious to water. Repeat every two years.* ▸ *Wicker furniture will break down immediately if it comes into contact with the weather.* ▸ *Garden benches make the perfect places to enjoy your masterpiece.* ▸ *Wrought iron should be painted and softened with cushions.* ▸ *Found items like these painted spades go with a beach theme.*

LEFT: A classical nude. **RIGHT:** Gilded arum-like leaves are strong forms mirrored here in the water below.

Unless you like chaos and clutter, try not to overload the garden with too many items, they will quickly lose their impact. Some simple tricks include thinking of the elements of scale, placement and material. Experiment with macro and miniature scale – this leads to a variety of experiences. Do you want to touch the sculpture to add to the sensory experience? If so place it somewhere the visitor doesn't have to walk over garden beds to reach. Overlap sculpture with water to create complete pictures. Do you want the ornament to tell a story? Small sculptural surprises can be linked together along your garden journey. Whatever you choose, sculpture can change with time, mood and style and at the end of the day it's the easiest thing to change and manipulate to create a different vibe, so just give it a go and experiment.

GARDEN FURNITURE

Keep the furniture simple and uncluttered and let the rest of the garden do the magic. Tables and chairs should be functional and simple elements that lead to greater enjoyment, rather than seen as features. Outdoor furniture comes in a range of materials, each differing in lifespan and maintenance requirements. Hardwood timbers, such as teak and jarrah, are hard wearing, while wicker and cane are shorter lived. Stay away from timber furniture made of tropical hardwoods as they exploit our forest resources. Metal furniture, such as powder-coated, cast and wrought iron, will never date but is often uncomfortable without soft cushions, and you know it's all about comfort. The

Try shopping at one of the auctioneers or country fairs around town. You may find something that not only suits your budget but is unique.

LEFT: *Painting timber furniture will increase its life.*

choice of outdoor furniture can be overwhelming and expensive. I like to hunt around auctions and local fairs for interesting and less expensive options. Again, choose furniture on the basis of how it fits in with other materials in the garden and remember to try before you buy. I have often sat in an uncomfortable seat and wondered how could you live with a seat you don't want to sit on!

To narrow your selection, ask yourself the following questions:

▶ How many people do you need to seat?
▶ What is your budget?
▶ Will the furniture need to be weatherproof?
▶ Will you need to move it around?
▶ What style will suit your garden design?

LIGHTING

Lighting will extend the pleasure of your garden well into the night. Use it in your entertaining area for a nocturnal dinner party or to highlight an accent tree or plant grouping. Lighting can also be used to subtly enhance an existing focal point as well as creating new more intangible ones. Consider illuminating a feature that would otherwise go unnoticed, such as the boughs of an ornamental tree, the shadows of foliage against a wall or the ripple of water in a pond. As the garden fades to black, other elements will come alive, adding a further dimension and another surprise.

Use a low-voltage lighting system for ease and safety. Low voltage lighting utilises a transformer that should be located inside or protected from the elements. The cable can be quite safely placed below the mulch close to the surface but should be protected in a sheath. Low voltage is only limited by distance; anything over 30 metres will need a transformer fed by mains electricity or by using a number of low voltage circuits around the garden. If you require a large system, employ a lighting designer and electrician, and make it your first priority before constructing the garden. Oh and remember electrical light systems will need maintenance albeit rarely, so place your lights where you can reach them to change a globe.

Look out for the great range of solar garden lights available. I found a hanging temple light that has small solar panels on top of the light fixture and is simply inserted into the soil with a spike. It casts an eerie blue moonlike light as soon as it gets dark. I love the idea that it doesn't use electricity (so I never have to worry about children or pets) and is completely movable. I can use them to line a pathway one night or surround the dance floor (that is my outdoor pavilion) for an evening birthday celebration the next night.

Installing electricity

Do you need electricity for a pumped water feature, lawn mower or lighting system? It's a good idea to get an electrician to install this first. Think carefully about the placement of the outdoor electricity outlet, better to position cables along boundaries where digging will be kept to a minimum. Electricity cables should be buried in trenches 60–100 cm beneath the ground. Record the line of the trenches and cables on your site plan.

planting

A great garden is much more than just the plants. In fact, plants are relatively low on the list of elements when it comes to designing your garden, and certainly they are one of the last components to be put in. However, plants often are relied upon to create the mood, atmosphere and the volume in a garden. I concede some people are more plant orientated than others — each to their own. Once you understand the concept of nurturing a plant you will have it for life. We all have our own individual style and entity, and this can easily translate into a living canvas. Whether a garden has a mass planting of one species or is a living patchwork quilt of colour, planting should respond to the owner and make a statement.

What follows will help you create a livable and triumphant contemporary garden. Make a list of all the functions that your plants will need to perform, and then choose plants based on performance, vigour, resistance to disease and maintenance requirements. If you do this now, you will never waste money on the wrong plant, nor will you have to remove a plant later on. Resist buying a plant on impulse, as it will rarely fit into the scheme of things, and end up being a waste of money. Conversely, I must state that some people can never say no to a new plant, and always fit 'just another one in'. I call these 'plant people'; they tend to spend their weekends traipsing around nurseries looking for that elusive specimen. And even though I'm related to people like this, I try to avoid the impulse buy.

ABOVE: *Rosemary Verey's winning combination is much loved and consistently repeated.*

List the functions each plant needs to fulfil:

1. A shade tree, deciduous, flowering, wide canopy and grows to 5 m.
2. Hedge grows to 2 m, flowering, evergreen, thick foliage.
3. Feature tree, 6 m high, pyramidal shape, spring flowers, autumn foliage and interesting bark.
4. Accent plant, bold form, grows to 1 metre, straplike foliage,
5. A flower display, spring and summer flowers, white, blue, lime and lemon, low maintenance.

Keep the following in mind when choosing your plants: their requirements, impact, seasonality, perfume and form. Group plants that need similar requirements together, for example keep hot dry lovers together. A common mistake is to place plants with different water requirements together.

BELOW: *Tough, stylish and unkillable, the New Zealand flax is top of my list for impact and textual contrast.*

PLANTING TO CREATE IMPACT

Whatever the style of your garden, whatever your theme and whatever your choices, the goal should be to achieve impact. Don't be content with half measures. Good planting requires a simple goal and full execution. For a bold garden bed, plant hundreds of the same type of plant. If you want a kaleidoscope of colour, like a magic carpet, plant large drifts or blocks of the same type of plant. If you are looking for a forest feel, then plant the same tree in all different sizes to give immediate impact. The use of accent plants, such as New Zealand flax, clipped spheres and topiary standards, will lead to a bold design that will maintain the framework and form throughout the year. Simplify the garden by limiting the plant material. This will help to create a more unified garden and will also cut down on the maintenance. Repeating the same plant will create rhythm and cohesion.

PLANTING IN LAYERS

Graduating heights of plantings from the tallest at the back to the smallest at the front will create a full, well-sculpted garden, and a feeling of enclosure. I like to think of it as planting in layers. The first layer consists of the border plants that define the edge. The second layer, has slightly larger plants, building up the further into the garden you go. The next layer comprises the canopy of overhanging smaller trees and larger shrubs. This canopy creates overhead enclosure and a feeling of security. Taller trees are the final layer; essential for birdlife and maintaining dappled microclimates in your garden. Planting in layers applies to large gardens, courtyards and even potted plants.

Tip: Apply the rule of planting in layers to containers and you will create a complete garden.

ABOVE: *Christopher Lloyd's Great Dixter is a great example of planting in layers. His perennial borders make full use of height, form and flower shape.* BELOW: *Choose thyme, woolly thyme or lemon thyme for a soft and fragrant seat.*

PLANTING FOR PERFUME

Fragrances evoke emotions and strong links to memories. Flowers, leaves, even the scent of a newly mowed lawn can enrich your outdoor experience. Fragrance enhances the spirit of place, creating a real sense of the present as well as links to the past. Fragrances range from fresh daytime scents to sweeter nocturnal scents. So no matter what your taste, there is a fragrance for you. Sweet scents like the invisible *Osmanthus fragrans* smells just like apricot bars. Violets are sensational fragrant groundcovers, while you can't beat gardenia for its fresh lemon aroma. Pretty bouquet perfumes of roses, lavender and heliotrope are great in sunny spots. Nocturnal scents of 'Angel's Trumpet' (*Brugmansia*), 'Port Wine Magnolia' (*Michelia figo*), 'Moonflower' (*Ipomoea alba*) and 'Night Scented Stock' (*Matthiola bicornis*) are barely noticeable during the day but intense at night. I like planting them beneath bedroom windows to enjoy all night long. I also like walking the dog at night and trying to guess what fragrance I can smell. Plant herbs, such as lemon verbena, mint and thyme along paths and in pots so visitors can brush against them to release their fresh fragrances. Oh and before I forget, there's nothing like walking in the rain and picking up a whiff of the lemon scented myrtle (*Backhousia citriodora*), as the rain drops release the oils in the leaves.

CONTRAST PLANT FORM AND TEXTURE

Look at the diversity of plant and flower forms. Flowers come in all sizes and give the most impact when used together. Tall and elegant floral spires, umbel inflorescences, bell-shaped flowers, large trumpet flowers as well as delicate sprays of flowers all contribute to the immense variety of a floral display. Look at the shapes of trees and shrubs too. They come in every shape and size: cones, umbrellas, spires, buns, pyramids and columns. For example the frangipani has a well-known rounded umbrella-shaped canopy whilst palms have shaggy shaped leaf fronds that contrast well with one another. Italian cypresses have tall elegant spires, which work well with the rounded buns of the olive canopy. Strap-leaved flax are often key ingredients that contrast brilliantly against tighter and smaller textured shrubs. By placing contrasting plant forms next to each other you attract attention. You are able to really define the living environment. Symmetrical plant-

LEFT: *Use different flower shapes to create a picture. Tall hollyhock spires intermingle with clusters of rampant roses.*
RIGHT: *Flat heads of lemon yarrow (**Achillea**) work well against the rising globes of the ornamental onion (**Allium**).*

64

ings and topiary will lend to the formality of the garden and can be contrasted with more chaotic flower beds to create drama and interest.

Accent plants, such as yucca, agave, cacti, grass trees, palms, flax and ornamental grasses, create foliage focal points. Plant en masse to create massive impact or use individually to attract attention. Be careful they don't totally dominate the space. Remember less is often more.

PLANTING COLOURS

Think of your garden as a canvas for your own individual artistic expression. A garden picture is formed gradually by using clever combinations and enough of the same type of plant to create broad brushstrokes of colour across the canvas. The only rule to remember when choosing colourful planting combinations is to

Topiary is impressive but a constant chore.

LEFT: *The strong form of the agave is contrasted against the softness of flowers.* **MIDDLE:** *The sculptural form of the Jerusalem artichoke attracts attention.* right: *Textural contrast between grass, daisy and seaholly catches the eye.*

CLOCKWISE FROM TOP LEFT: *Strong lines of palm trunks create texture and rhythm* ▶ *Keep in mind the beauty of bark.* ▶ *Flowers come and go but foliage lasts for ever* ▶ *Who minds if the* **Calathea pseudo veichiana** *never flowers?* ▶ **Stachys** *'Big Ears' has leaves so furry and soft, they make you want to reach out to stroke them.*

select plants that flower at the same time. Opt for putting plants together that like moist shade, put hot-dry lovers together and so on. Once you've chosen the colour combinations and the picture you want to paint, scour nurseries and garden catalogues for suitable plants that do their thing at the same time.

There are so many colours within a garden and they change so dramatically over the course of a year. For example, the flower colour of the 'Iceplant' (*Sedum spectabilis*) will change at least three times through the year, the buds start out as lime green at the beginning of summer, opening up slowly to intense pink then fading to a rusty brown during autumn.

SEASONAL PLANTING

Choose plants that perform well in more than one season of the year. For example, if you have space for only one small tree, select a tree that has brilliant autumn

66

colour, spring flowers, great wintry bark and terrific summer shade. Discover the seasonal responses of a plant before you choose it. Why wait a year for a display that will last only two weeks? The more research you do, the more choices you will have. Each design included in this book has five plant profiles; these plants have been selected on the basis that they perform in more than one season.

Plants for windy areas

Windy spots need specific plant solutions. Look to the coastline of Australia for inspiration. Windbreaks can be essential elements in areas of high wind and will help make outdoor areas more livable. Plant the windbreak with a variety of foliage sizes and different heights to help provide a strong impenetrable barrier.

- ▶ Coastal banksia (*Banksia serrata*)
- ▶ *Cordyline terminalis*
- ▶ Dragon tree (*Dracaena draco*)
- ▶ Giant yucca (*Yucca* species)
- ▶ Mirror bush (*Coprossma repens* 'Pink Splendor', 'Gold Splash')
- ▶ New Zealand Christmas tree (*Metrosideros excelsior*)
- ▶ Pink/red flax (*Phormium* 'Rainbow Warrior')
- ▶ Purple flax (*Phormium tenax* 'Purpureum', 'Dazzler')

Water plants

- ▶ Arum Lily (*Zandedeschia aethiopica*)
- ▶ Giant ornamental rhubarb (*Gunnera maculata*)
- ▶ Papyrus (*Cyperus papyrus*)
- ▶ Water lilies (*Nymphaea* hybrids)
- ▶ Water Iris (*Iris pseudacorus*)
- ▶ Water poppy (*Hydrocleys nymphoides*)

Short-lived colour

Annual plants can be replaced each season to give terrific displays of colour all year round. Use them to decorate the garden for a special occasion or just for a change between the seasons. Limit plant choice and colour palette to highlight certain areas and bring the garden into your home by planting in pots around the house. Use vigorous and long flowering annuals to colour your garden. Select from the hundreds of great varieties of petunias, pansies, poppies, primulas, everlasting daisies, snapdragons, lobelias, tore-nias, geraniums and Sturt's Desert Pea. The nurseries will have single colours in stock, making it easier to colour code your garden. Keep annuals flowering longer by picking spent blooms and feeding with Thrive for Flowering Plants.

> Choose plants which are suitable to your particular climate. A plant growing out of its natural climate, for example, a Japanese flowering cherry in Sydney, will never perform well. It will tend to be troubled with diseases, insects and lack of vigour.

FROM LEFT TO RIGHT: *Decorative poppy seed heads are an ephemeral late spring surprise ▶ Waterlilies love to grow in water of about 40 cm depth ▶ Hyacinths provide short-term colour but the perfume will linger in your memory forever.*

containers

Don't forget the impact that can be made with pots. Pots and containers make the garden portable. They also assist in bringing the garden into paved areas, courtyards and balconies. A potted plant becomes an instant focal point and can soften a blank wall, emphasise a doorway or stairs and accentuate a corner. Containers can be large and dominant, or unobtrusive, small and repeated for effect. The type of container you choose should fit into the overall look and the materials you have used in the garden. Wine barrels, terracotta pots, metal buckets, stone planters and even plough disks can all be used to create a brilliant effect.

'I see my potted plants at my front door as friends — so welcoming and friendly and loyal, day after day — except in summer of course where their demands are far greater.' Christopher Lloyd, Great Dixter, East Sussex

Think of your pots as friends. The more affection they get from you, the more magic they will add to your life. Use a good quality potting mix with the Australian standards ticked on the bag. These potting mixes include water retention crystals and controlled release fertiliser to keep your potted plants looking sensational. Do not neglect your potted friends, keep them looking their best by root pruning every three years and topping up their nutrients twice a year. Watering is the main problem with potted plants, so choose tough drought hardy varieties or hook them up to your irrigation system. Most of us go off on holiday during the hottest part of the year, so make sure you don't return to a graveyard of plant corpses. Before you leave put your pots on the coolest side of the house, cover with shade cloth and use saucers beneath to trap any moisture. Ask a reliable friend to pop in and check on them regularly.

CHOOSING PLANTS FOR POTS

Some plants are better suited to pots than others. They can provide a sculptural focal point within the garden or become the garden on the balcony of an apartment where space is limited. Everyone has a spot for a pot! Make sure your pots do better than just survive, ensure they thrive by choosing wisely. Observe the area first; understand the patterns of sun and shade, and then research which plants will suit the spot. Remember that all potted plants are under stress from a reduced root-growth zone and fewer available nutrients. Multi-plant your pots to create your own mini garden.

OPPOSITE TOP: *Half wine barrels are perfect for bay trees, citrus and weeping maples.*
OPPOSITE BOTTOM: *Antique coppers add interest to a garden.*
ABOVE LEFT: *Flax and succulents make a striking combination in a hot spot.*
ABOVE: *Glazed ceramic pots give a dash of colour.*
LEFT: *Collect old terracotta pots but seal them first. The shrub here is the native hibiscus.*

LONG-TERM POT PLANTS

Long lasting plants like shrubs and small trees can last for years in pots. When mature specimens are grouped together in a courtyard they create an instant impression. A shady garden is cooling, restful and serene, but don't expect a riot of colour. Go for a lush sylvan scene of hosta, ferns, rhododendron or cycads. If you're looking for a small tree, try a Japanese maple, particularly the gorgeous red-stemmed 'Coral Barked Maple' (*Acer palmatum* 'Senkaki'). Other shade lovers include bird nest fern, 'Maiko' *Hydrangea*, *Camellia* 'Scentuous' and lilly pillies. In areas beneath a large tree, where root competition is rife, potted plants may be the only solution. Other suggestions for sunny spots include 'Little Gem' magnolia (*Magnolia grandiflora*). I just love the rusty brown reverse to their leaf and their enormous lemon scented blooms. Dwarf Chinese elm 'Frosty' has a cute white fringe to the leaf. It makes a well-behaved potted specimen

plant but will need a large tub. Choose dracaena, olives, flax and yucca for hot dry spots.

Succulents are sensational; in fact they will grow and flower anywhere. Most of Australia has a dry sunny climate, perfect conditions for these interesting plants. They're so easy to grow, needing virtually no attention and definitely no water! The choice of succulents in nurseries is huge; sculptures, tight rosettes, sprays, cascades and spines. They have smooth leaves, showy colours and grow just from one leaf! Succulents have shallow root systems, which are amazingly hardy and are able to withstand long periods of drought. Once you start a collection you will be hooked! Look out for my favourites ... the dramatic black rosettes of *Aeonium* 'Zwartkop', the frilly fancy pink foliage of echeveria and the huge sculptural form of the agaves. There is a new variety called 'Flapjacks', yes the leaves look like pikelets with their tips dipped in maroon paint.

CROPS IN POTS

Living in cities we have to make the most of our small living spaces. As a keen gardener who loves to cook, I plant my 'must have close' herbs near the back door. Brushing past them inspires me to think about food. Apartment living does not rule out growing your own salad crops and herbs. These edible plants can be grown in light polystyrene boxes, hydroponically and in pots. Harvest your own strawberries, repeat harvest lettuce, rocket, coriander, garlic, mint, chives, basil, parsley, oregano and chilli from your deck or balcony. A friend of mine grows strawberries in recycled gutters around the entire fence in the back garden, they trail and provide lush sweet berries all summer long. Fresh, close and organic — what more could you want? Citrus grow well in tubs too; orange, lemons and limes will bear fruit when fed every three months with a pelleted manure.

INDOOR POT PLANTS

Plants indoors help reduce the stress of daily life and provide a serene and relaxing environment. Select rounded leaf forms and smooth leaves, as plants like this have good feng shui. Plants like Madonna lily, raphis palms, bird nest ferns and diffenbachia will contribute to a luscious harmonious indoor environment. *Spathyphyllum* 'Sensation' has huge voluptuous leaves that must be kept shining. In a bright room you will get lovely white 'lily-like' flowers. Raphis palms are the Rolls Royce of houseplants. A large glossy clump of raphis makes a great statement in any room. *Diffenbachia* 'Tropic Marianne' is a trendy, textural and dramatic indoor plant that loves to show its wild lime foliage up against a blank wall. Stay away from spiky plants like cacti, as they are annoying to bump into and can create tension indoors.

► Birds nest fern (*Asplenium australasicum*)
► Bromeliad (*Aechmea, Vriesea*)

OPPOSITE: *Add eternal style and flair with rosette succulents such as the dramatic* **aeoniums.**
ABOVE: *Intermingle salad crops with herbs and ensure they are within picking distance of the kitchen.*

► Cast iron plant (*Aspidistra elatior*)
► Croton (*Codiaeum variegatum* 'America', 'Petra')
► *Ctenanthe* 'Silver Star'
► Dumb cane (*Dieffenbachia seguine* 'Tropic Marianne')
► Fiddleleaf fig (*Ficus lyrata*)
► Golden cane palms (*Chrysalidocarpus lutescens*)
► Lady palm (*Rhapis excelsa*)
► *Philodendron* 'Xanadu'

71

▸ Peace or Madonna lily (*Spathiphyllum* 'Sensation')

▸ Striped elephant's ear (*Alocasia x amazonica*)

▸ Tree philodendron (*Philodendron bipinnatifidum*)

CARNIVOROUS PLANTS IN POTS

Carnivorous plants like venus flytraps, sundews and pitcher plants grow well in pots but need to sit in water. The best spot for them is a bright windowsill or sunny courtyard with a deep saucer filled with rainwater. They'll love keeping your kitchen windowsill free from flies and mosquitoes whilst providing beautiful flowers and forms. I find venus flytraps are especially intriguing for small children and a good way to get them interested in gardening.

TOP POTS

When gardening on a balcony, use tough plants that will cope with the strong winds. Determine the direction and velocity of winds. Reduce the effects of prevailing winds by putting up a clear Perspex screen, this way you won't interfere with views. Other useful screens include 'Natureed', lattice and bamboo fencing. Plant a living screen in troughs if you need to reduce winds and block unwanted

ABOVE: *Look out for interesting foliage to liven indoors, Ctenanthe 'Silver Star'.*

views. My favourite plants for screening include golden bamboo for a touch of the orient. Looks great in a glazed ceramic pot. Sacred bamboo (*Nandina domestica*) is not a true bamboo but will quickly provide a thick screen of ferny foliage with its large compound leaf. This tough screening plant will grow to 3 metres and also provide sprays of starry white flowers followed by clusters of red berries.

Sculptural plants for pots

▸ *Aeonium arboreum* 'Zwartkop'

▸ Cabbage tree (*Cordyline australis*)

▸ Century plant (*Agave attenuata*)

▸ Cycad (*Cycas revoluta*)

▸ *Dracaena marginata*

▸ Grass tree (*Xanthorrhoea australis*)

▸ Mother-in-law's tongue (*Sansevieria trifasciata* 'Laurentii')

▸ Spanish bayonet (*Yucca* spp.)

Pot plants for hot spots

▸ *Aeonium arboreum* 'Zwartkop'

▸ Angel's trumpet (*Brugsmania* 'Frosty Pink')

▸ Chinese star jasmine (*Trachelospermum jasminoides*)

▸ *Cordyline australis*

▸ *Cotyledon orbiculata*

▸ *Crassula* 'Gollum', 'Hobbit'

▸ Common houseleek (*Sempervivum tectorum*)

▸ *Echeveria* hybrids 'Black Prince', 'Violet Queen', 'Afterglow'

▸ Frangipani (*Plumeria* hybrids)

▸ Geranium (*Pelargonium* ivy leafed and zonal hybrids)

▸ Grass tree (*Xanthorrhoea australis*)

▸ Lavender (*Lavendula* 'Sidonie', 'Pukehou')

▸ Magnolia 'Little Gem'

▸ Mother-in-law's tongue (*Sansevieria trifasciata* 'Laurentii')

▶ Olive (*Olea europaea subsp. Europaea*)

▶ Oranges/lemons (*Citrus* spp.)

▶ Protea (*Protea* 'Blushing Bride')

▶ Thread edged agave (*Agave filifera*)

▶ White dwarf agapanthus (*Agapanthus* 'Snowstorm')

▶ Yucca (*Yucca elephantipes*)

Pot plants for shady places

▶ Angel wing begonia (*Begonia* 'Pink Shasta')

▶ Arum lily (*Zantedeschia aethiopica*)

▶ Brazilian bell flower (*Abutilon* spp.)

▶ Bromeliads (*Vreisea, Neoregelia, Billbergia*)

▶ Camellia (*Camellia japonica* 'Lovelight', 'Early Pearly', 'Scentuous')

▶ Coleus (*Solenostemon scutellarioides* cultivars)

▶ Fringe flower (*Lorapetalum chinensis* 'China Pink')

▶ Fuchsia (*Fuchsia* hybrids)

▶ Gardenia (*Gardenia florida*, G. 'Magnifica', 'Prof. Pucci', 'True Love')

▶ Japanese aralia (*Fatsia japonica*)

▶ Japanese maple (*Acer japonicum dissectum*)

▶ Lamium (*Lamium* 'White Nancy')

▶ Native water fern (*Blechnum nudum*)

▶ New Guinea impatiens

▶ Peacock bush (*Calathea makoyana*)

▶ September lily (*Clivia miniata* hybrids)

Pot plants for flower colour

▶ Azaleas (*Rhododendron azalea kurume* hybrids)

▶ Dwarf bougainvillea (*Bougainvillea* 'Bambino' hybrids)

▶ *Dipladenia* (*Mandevilla* 'Alice du Pont', 'White Fantasy', 'Red Fantasy')

▶ Geraniums (*Pelargonium* ivy leafed and zonal hybrids)

▶ Bougainvillea (*Bougainvillea glabra* 'Magnifica' and bambino hybrids)

▶ Verbena (*Verbena Kanzan* hybrids)

ABOVE LEFT: *Sculptural cycads make a strong focal point.* **ABOVE RIGHT:** *Add a handful of sulphate of potash to keep bougainvilleas flowering.* **BELOW:** *Succulents are a gardener's best friend. When a leaf falls off put it back in the pot and it will spring into life.*

TYPES OF CONTAINERS

You can tell so much about a person by looking at their outdoor living areas ... twin sandstone urns filled with flax, a group of oriental cobalt glazed pots or a row of geranium filled old boots. The type of container and where it's placed remains just as personal as the design of the garden. Choose from this huge range of containers to decorate your outdoor living areas to add flair, fun, excitement and to focus attention. A glazed ceramic bowl brimming with clear water adds the sparkle of fish to the arrangement.

Ceramic

Ceramic pots are durable, colourful and can quickly dress up an outside area. Bright glazes work well outdoors; shiny glossy surfaces combine with foliages to reflect garden light. Ceramic pots suit the tropical look.

Metal

Modernise your garden by using metallic pots like copper, stainless steel and iron. Try using other lightweight surfaces coated in metallic spray. Repeat stainless steel buckets along a wall to give your garden a modern look. Try planting variegated mother-in-law's tongue in the buckets. It's vertical striped leaves give a dramatic effect. An old recycled copper makes a good planter; it soon weathers to verdigris green with exposure to oxygen and water. Cast iron is perfect for classical gardens with a touch of formality. Cast iron urns are expensive so look out for faux plastic ones — trust me, no one will know the difference until they lift it!

Lightweight plastic pots

Plastic pots are made to resemble cast iron, sandstone and terracotta. Some even have a textured finish for added realism. They are light, easy to move, cheap and durable, perfect for some balconies that

ABOVE: *Flower-ball baskets are very romantic. Cascading* **verbena,** *daisy and* **nemesia** *drip all summer long.*

should only carry plastic planters, as others are too heavy. Place them on castor wheels to make them even easier to move.

Terracotta

Terracotta pots come in all shapes and sizes, from traditional to contemporary. Mass produced lines are inexpensive but are rarely water or frost proof, so remember to seal them to prevent moisture being sucked out of the potting mix. The larger sized terracotta pots are usually handmade. I cram my collection of terracotta pots full of everything I can find that is hardy, colourful and easy to grow.

Stone

Stone pots and troughs are expensive and heavy, however, they do add a touch of class. In time they weather and become covered in moss and lichen. A simple stone bowl will make a Japanese garden, and a classic stone planter makes for a fine focus in a formal herb circle.

Timber

The best example of a timber container is the Versailles planter. They were traditionally used for citrus and palm trees at Versailles so they could be moved inside the Orangery for winter. They look best planted with topiary, citrus, palms, lollipops and spirals. Stain or paint them to match with your colour scheme. Half wine barrels are versatile and large enough to grow good-sized plants. To repot, place the container on its side. Shave 5–10 cm off the exposed root ball with a bread knife and infill with new potting mix.

Bargain

Look out for recycled and junk containers to plant things in. You'll be amazed how much money you will save and you are assured it will be unique. I love using old coppers, quirky aluminum cans, junky colanders, plough disks, enamel buckets, antique chimney pots, old boots, watering cans and wheelbarrows to give a garden an individual touch.

Quick Tips

- Seal terracotta pots with a pot seal spray to reduce moisture loss.
- Always use good quality potting mix with the Australian standards tick on the bag.
- Add water storage crystals and water retention granules to protect your plants from the summer heat.
- Feed your plants regularly with controlled release fertiliser every six months as nutrient leaches out quickly and needs to be constantly replaced.
- Remember they are friends — repot them every two years with fresh potting mix and they will reward you.
- Never feed a sick plant, just water fortnightly with seaweed solution and work out what's causing the problem.
- Don't leave your pots standing in water. Allow plants to dry out before the next watering.
- Place pots on pot feet to allow the soil to drain freely.
- Make sure your pot has a large drainage hole. Nothing kills a plant faster than wet feet.
- Fill small pots with seasonal potted colour, this is cheaper than a bunch of flowers and lasts longer.
- Wash pots thoroughly with hot water and a scrubbing brush when repotting.

CARING FOR YOUR POTTED FRIENDS

Potted plants are much more demanding than plants in the garden. They have different water requirements throughout the year. Some pots will require twice daily watering in the summer and every two weeks in the winter. Always check the soil moisture about 8 cm beneath the surface. In winter, water plants only when the soil dries out. If they are kept moist all the time they will freeze or drown. Add seaweed solution to sweeten up the soil, it's a tonic not a fertiliser. Easy-to-assemble home irrigation kits can be used to water all your pot plants with a turn of the tap. A drip or trickle irrigation system will deliver water precisely where the plant needs it and minimises evaporation

Plants grown in containers will need a specialised controlled release fertiliser. Add a spoonful of granules to the top of the soil every three months. To promote and prolong flowering, water them with a water-soluble fertiliser, for example Thrive for Flowering Plants or Garden Gold are great for this purpose. Deadhead spent blooms to encourage a new flush of flowers. This will keep the plant looking neat and fresh. Tip pruning will keep the plants looking bushy and pushing on with lateral growth. When the plant reaches its maximum size for its allotted space, it risks becoming pot bound. You then have two choices. You can repot into a larger size pot or you can trim the root ball by removing up to 10 cm of the matted roots around the perimeter. This will allow you to fill the space with fresh potting mix and a sprinkle of slow release fertiliser.

inspire
romantic

Flower beds brim with soft pastel blooms. Fragrances hang still in the air. Butterflies dip their wings in aerial pursuit. Enclose yourself with roses and feel free to dream.

If you adore romance then you can't go past a rose garden. Cottage gardens and flower gardens may need a little more effort and attention, but they will reward your labour tenfold by giving you endless flowers that smell so sweet. The perfume of a romantic garden becomes imprinted on memory — remember the sweet violets that your grandmother grew.

What is it about roses? The opulent petal arrangement and their strong, heady perfume seem to send us wild. Whether you want a garden billowing with flowers, a love bench, soft roses and a romantic pavilion for two or a secluded swinging garden seat, it's easy to create a dreamy romantic garden. Add lighting and the evening perfumes will extend the romance well into the night.

romantic cottage garden

GARDEN DESIGN PLAN

The symmetrical layout of this garden matches the architecture of the weatherboard cottage. Traditional rose gardens have a formal layout using a simple circular geometry. The rose garden originated in England. The garden beds have been designed to contain roses and the billowing nature of perennials. A system of circular pathways creates the garden journey and revolves around the heart of the garden. Each path terminates at a resting spot. A rose arbor and bench invites you to sit and relax. The clipped hedges around each garden bed accentuate the formality of the design. The intersecting paths create two main vistas, one from the rose arbor to the house, and the other from the bench to the sculpture.

PLANTING KEY
1. Crepe Myrtle
2. Luma apiculata
3. Roses & assorted perennials
4. Climbing roses & clematis
5. Formally clipped cone topiary
6. Low hedge, Lonicera
7. Kitchen gardens

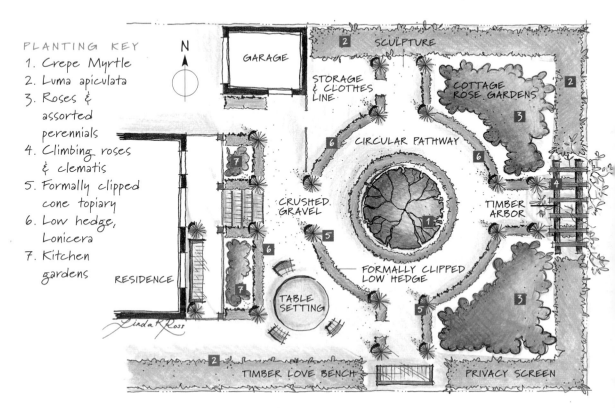

DESIGN TRICKS

By using a cross axis we divide the garden into quad-rants, creating more interesting pathways. The sym-metry adds formality to the cottage garden.

By planting a small tree in the centre of the gar-den, we give the garden a living heart.

By ending each vista with a focal point, we add to the ways we can personalise our garden places. In this case a sculpture, a pergola and a love bench.

SUITABLE CLIMATES

Arid, temperate and cold zones

PLANTING SCHEME

Pastels and perfumes are notable in this garden. Perennials are planted en masse in drifts, graduating from taller plants at the back to smaller ones in the front. Select English roses for this garden, they are modern roses bred with old-fashioned forms and fra-grances. Their blooms have more petals than hybrid tea climbing roses, forming a loose quartered rose arrangement. Roses mixed with clematis cascade over arbors, while a clipped hedge attempts to contain the billowing clouds of perennials and roses.

OPPOSITE: *Plant coneflowers, lamb's ear and salvia in drifts.* **ABOVE LEFT:** *Define the circle with neat clipped hedges to contain roses and cottage plants. Mark each entrance with cone-shaped topiaries.* **ABOVE RIGHT:** *Pretty poppies are the belles of the ball.* **BELOW:** *Create a garden journey with dissecting paths. Gravel surfaces are especially suitable for cottage gardens.*

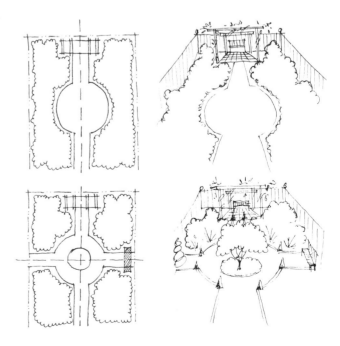

planting list

- Agapathus (*Agapathus* 'Purple Cloud')
- Box honeysuckle (*Lonicera nitida*)
- Butterfly bush (*Buddleia davidii*)
- Catmint (*Nepeta x faasenii*)
- Cherry pie (*Heliotropium arborescens* 'Cherry Pie')
- Crepe myrtle (*Lagerstroernia*)
- *Diascia* 'Blackthorn Apricot'
- Ice plant (*Sedum spectabile*)
- Lamb's ears (*Stachys byzantina*)
- Oriental lily (Lilium, oriental hybrids)
- *Penstemon* 'Apple Blossom'
- Pokers (*Kniphofia* hybrids)
- Poppy (*Papaver* hybrids)
- Purple coneflower (*Echinacea purpurea*)
- *Rosa* 'Pat Austin', 'Graham Thomas', 'Burgundy Iceberg'
- Russian sage (*Perovskia atriplicifolia*)
- Seaside daisy (*Erigeron* hybrids)
- Shasta daisy (*Leucanthemum x superbum*)
- *Verbascum* 'Helen Johnson'
- Virgin's bower (*Clematis*)
- Windflowers (*Anenome* hybrids)
- Wormwood (*Artemesia* 'Powis Castle')
- Yarrow (*Achillea cultivars*)

GARDEN ART

I personalised this garden by making my own sculptures. Brolgas dance above a cloud of flowers in the perennial beds. Imagine spotting two graceful brolgas from the corner of your eye resting within the woodland. The birds are built from smooth river stones and reinforced steel. Select smooth river boulders for the body. Mark and drill holes into the centre of the boulder for the neck and legs. Twist and bend reinforcement to create the legs and an arched neck. Dry fit to ensure you're happy with curves and the illusion of movement. Glue into place with exterior waterproof glue. Glue air bromeliads (*Tillandsia*) onto each side of the body for living wings. *Tillandsia* are bromeliads that feed off the moisture in the air, so mist occasionally with water .

Attracting butterflies

A cottage garden is not complete without butterflies. Their pretty wings are pure joy. These plants are guaranteed to bring in clouds of butterflies.

- *Spider flower (Cleome)*
- *Orchids assorted*
- *Easter daisy (Aster hybrids)*
- *Butterfly bush (Buddleia)*
- *Escallonia hybrids*
- *Ice plant (Sedum spectabilis)*
- *Wattles (Acacia)*

Seaside daisy

Rose 'Burgundy Iceberg'

Clematis

Japanese windflower

Crepe myrtle

Windflower

81

plant profiles

 height & width of plant

 good for pot

 prefers full sun

 prefers partial shade

 tolerates full shade

 frost hardy

 frost tender

LEFT: *The new Indian summer range of crepe myrtles are resistant to powdery mildew.* **RIGHT:** *Windflowers are easy to grow.*

CREPE MYRTLE (INDIAN SUMMER RANGE)
Lagerstroemia indica

     varied height 5 m X 3 m

suitable for a large tub
crepe flowers, smooth bark and autumn foliage

What a trifecta! This medium-sized tree has great summer flowers, autumn foliage and interesting smooth bark in winter. Crepe myrtles are more resistant to powdery mildew than the older varieties and come in a range of heights and colours including pink, lilac, magenta and white. The flowers resemble frilly crepe paper. An open attractive canopy shape will result if the tree is not pruned.

WINDFLOWERS
Anenome x hybrids

    1.2 m x 1 m

clouds of white flowers

Breathtaking in autumn, I love how windflowers gently sway in the breeze. They are an easy perennial to grow as they will look after themselves. Perfect for partly shaded areas, windflowers come in pure white, light pink and cerise. Plants remain as a dense ground cover growing to 40 cm until they flower, the flowers will then extend up to 1.5 m.

> Sprinkle with cow manure to encourage large clumps

VIRGIN'S BOWER
Clematis large flower hybrids

    3 m x 1 m

wonderful flowers; dislike humidity

The clematis climbs by twisting tendrils along a support. They love a cooler climate and need a cool root zone with good moisture retention. Their huge,

FROM LEFT TO RIGHT: *Clematis need a cool climate. Coneflowers flower for months. Lamb's ears flower in cool climates.*

plate-sized flowers adorn the climber in spring followed by fluffy seed heads through winter. Clematis love to grow into the sun while the roots stay cool in the shade, so plant them just inside an arch or at the base of another plant. Flowers come in blues, mauves, pinks and white. The roots can be shaded by planting it just inside the arch.

PURPLE CONEFLOWER
Echinacea purpurea

    1.2 m x 0.4 m

long-lived flower colour

Purple coneflower is a showy summer flowering perennial with huge, pointed daisy-like flowers that sit tall and proud. The dried roots are used in herbal medicine to increase the body's resistance to cold and flu. Look out for new smaller varieties, 'Kim's Knee High' and 'Kim's Mops Head'. Divide the rhi-

zome from winter to early spring only if you need more plants, otherwise leave them be. Echinacea needs rich fertile soil and doesn't like to be moved around. Deadhead old flowers to encourage new ones. Plant around the veggies to attract the bees.

LAMB'S EARS
Stachys byzantina

     0.5 m x 0.4 m

showy silver foliage

This showy silver groundcover has soft and furry leaves. The silvery-grey foliage makes this a good contrast plant in a perennial garden as it provides a rest for the eyes. Hardy and fairly drought tolerant, lamb's ears will quickly spread into a carpet of soft silver. 'Big Ears' has larger leaves with pretty pink spires of flowers in cool climates. Propagate lamb's ears by root division in late winter.

plant profiles

FROM LEFT TO RIGHT: *Prop up huge heads of yarrow with tripods and perennial supports. 'Pat Austin' has magnificent blooms. 'Graham Thomas' will climb over anything.*

YARROW
Achillea 'Moonshine'

   0.6 m X 0.5 m

sulphur yellow flowers

Named after Achilles, who in Greek mythology healed wounds with this plant. Achilleas have hairy fern-like foliage and large flat heads of tiny daisy-like flowers. Flowers can be dried, as they hold their colour well. Propagate by division in late winter. Yarrow likes well drained soil. 'Moonshine' is more upright and has sulphur yellow flowers right through summer. It is a perfect companion for roses.

ROSES
Rosa 'Pat Austin', *Rosa* 'Burgundy Iceberg'

   1 m X 1 m

flush after flush of flowers

Shrub roses flower for nine months of the year when planted in six hours of sun per day. Pick the blooms and these roses will thank you by giving you a never ending supply. Feed with well rotted cow manure at the end of winter and mulch with lucerne hay.

CLIMBING ROSE
Rosa 'Graham Thomas'

   2 m X 1 m

clusters of lemon yellow roses

Climbing roses need only a sunny position and something to drape their bowers over. They might drift chaotically across a garden wall or an elegant iron framework, or cleverly hide an old stump or an ugly outhouse in a gorgeous riot of colour and perfume.

My favourite climbing rose was bred by David Austin in England and is called 'Graham Thomas', which is famous for its lemon clusters of fragrant flowers. Feed every three months

> Hold off pruning climbing roses until the second year. Establish the framework first, then cut back laterals to the main stems in winter.

with rotted cow manure and mulch well with lucerne hay. Other good climbing roses include 'Albertine', 'Climbing Iceberg', 'Pierre de Ronsard', 'Gold Bunny', 'Altissimo' and 'Sparrow's Hoop'. Some support is required when growing climbing roses on walls or fences. Firmly tie the rose framework onto horizontal wires.

FOCAL POINT

Arbors and arches are perfect features for a cottage rose garden. This rose arbor is a focal point to the long axis viewed from the back door. The pitch of the arbor roof matches the pitch of the house and is painted in the same Federation colours of cream and green. Remember to add a trellis or wire for the rose and clematis as a support. Select a sunny position for the arbor and plant vigorous perfumed climbers to grow over the arbor to soften the effect. Combine climbing roses with the evergreen Chinese star jasmine (*Trachelospermum jasminoides*), this will provide glossy green foliage in winter that will mask the the deciduous stems of the roses. Large-flowered hybrid clematis and white wisteria (*Wisteria sinensis* 'Alba') also make beautiful companions for climbing roses.

GARDEN CARE

Roses like hot, dry conditions. They tend to be plagued by fungal diseases in humid areas. Research has shown that spraying roses with a mixture of half water and half milk will prevent black spot and powdery mildew. Feed them often with well-rotted manures and mulch thickly with lucerne hay. Hose off aphids with a strong jet of water or apply a garlic spray. Spraying them with seaweed solutions will strengthen the cell walls, making the plants more resilient to disease.

Buy perennials from nurseries, purchase by mail order, sow them from seed or propagate them from cuttings. Plant into compost-enriched soil in high, mounded garden beds to increase drainage. Perennials are best planted in autumn when the soil is still warm to encourage root growth and the air is cooling down. During the warmer months, regularly remove spent flowers and foliage. Cut back leggy growth in autumn and water well. After several years the clump will enlarge and will be ready to divide. Dig out the clump or crown with a

ABOVE: *Perennial supports are helpful to prop up top heavy cottage plants.*

sharp spade, taking care not to damage any roots. Cut the root system into four and replant around the garden, adding compost as you go. Perennials look best grouped or in swathes. Fertilise perennials when they grow back in spring.

the potted cottage garden

Bring the cottege garden onto a balcony or into a sunny courtyard by filling a wine-barrel full of flowering cottage plants. Choose perennials, such as daisies, *Verbena*, *Felicia*, *Helichrysum* and *heliotrope* for colour, and then add ivy so it will spill over the sides of the barrel to soften the effect.

design

Your garden can go from predictable to sensational in one simple chapter. Keep the following design principles in mind, they are the secrets to your dream garden.

These principles are to get you thinking less like a gardener and more like a garden designer. The more you think in this way, the easier it will be to apply these rules or design concepts to your garden. Greater understanding of these design principles will lead to overall success by giving you the tools you need to create the garden you desire.

ABOVE: *Red walls and seats synchronise your ideas.*
LEFT: *A central fountain gives this garden a focus.*
BELOW: *Symmetrical pots, palms and plants tie this sunken courtyard together in a unified design.*

my secrets to spectacular garden design

SIMPLICITY

Keep the design simple — discard any unnecessary clutter and complexity. Strong ideas and a vibrant vision count for everything.

SYMMETRY AND UNITY

Some people crave symmetry and balance. I understand this, formal gardens look and feel great. To commence a balanced design, start by dividing your garden into quadrants. Use these lines to inform pathways and focal points. Mirror features, such as pots, plants and sculpture, to unify the design. I find asymmetrical designs usually more interesting as they achieve unity through the diagonal and offset positioning of elements.

TOP LEFT: *Paint cane chairs French provincial blue to match other features in the garden.* **RIGHT:** *Create impact by repeating the catmint as a border for this path. It's a simple and dynamic technique.* **BOTTOM LEFT:** *The perfect combination of design principles: symmetry, proportion and a focal point .*

FOCAL POINT

Focal points attract the eye, so place them where they draw your attention. Try not to let a focal point compete with any others in the same view, as this will only clutter your design and add confusion. Add them at the end of a vista, to be seen from a window, so as to lure you out of the house and into the garden. A focal point can be as simple or as dramatic as you desire — a simple pot, bench, sculpture, a gush of water, or perhaps a mirror to capture light and movement enhancing the perception of space. Light your focal point during the night, it will increase the impact.

REPETITION

Repeat materials throughout the garden. For example, if you choose brick paving in the front garden try to use it in the pathways that link the front with the back. Repeating a particular shape throughout the garden will create unity. Try drawing overlapping circles for the lawn, paving and a pond in your garden book. If you desire a circular garden design, mark the central point of your garden and then use a compass to draw concentric circles. Overlap another circle using a point along the larger circle as the central point for a new one. Another method is to cut out circles of paper and overlap them.

RHYTHM AND LINE

Use bold lines in garden design to give the garden a strong backbone. Whether you decide on a regimented formal design or a soft flowing design, the line will create movement and pattern. Use a sweeping line through your garden to create a simple but striking statement. Visual rhythm is important in a garden. Place items within the garden to create a repeated visual pattern so when viewed from afar they create a rhythm, like the notes in a piece of music. If you are wanting a flowing, relaxed garden design, hold the pencil lightly and let yourself go, allowing the pencil to move freely as you draw sweeping lines that ebb and flow. These can later evolve into pathways and garden beds.

TEXTURES

By placing different textures next to each other you will create more interest in your design. Large bold textures alongside long strap-like ones result in a dramatic display.

ABOVE: *Textual grasses move with the wind to create your garden's lifeforce.* **BELOW:** *These partly hidden stairs entice you to explore. Repetition of horizontal lines creates a certain rhythm. Steps should be a comfortable height, about 15 cm.*

ENERGY

Qi (pronounced chi) is an ancient Chinese principle of harnessing the life force. Energy is an intangible and ephemeral element within a garden, but vital if the garden is to have a life of its own. Choose textural grasses and strap-leafed plants that move with the breeze. They will bring a life force into the garden that you can feel moving within and around it. Encourage *qi* through flowing curved lines and softening harsh corners.

IMMERSE THE SENSES

Perfume, sound and touch are the intrinsic joys of a garden. They create what I call a further dimension, intangible but greatly rewarding.

SCALE AND PROPORTION

Ensure there is a balance between the sizes of the elements in your design. Sometimes an imbalance actually makes an exciting scene, such as a huge pot in a small courtyard. If you don't feel comfortable with this idea, choose perfectly proportioned elements that sit well within their own space. Playing around with different scales and proportions can be fun. Try experimenting with paper overlays placed on the photographs in your garden book.

SPACE, VOIDS AND VOLUMES

Think of your garden as a living sculpture. The garden will gradually grow, enlarge and evolve over time. Sculpt the space around your home with

plants. Create mass by building up volumes of planting and create essential voids by leaving vacant space , such as a lawn.

SYMBOLISM AND MEANING

What is important to you? Spiritual symbolism can be important in a garden but is tricky to get right. Seek information about the objects that you wish to include in your garden. Understand their inherent meaning in the culture from which they come and learn about their placement. For example, a frog is a symbol of happiness in a tropical Balinese garden. Cultural items, such as a Buddha carving or a Japanese stone lantern, have purpose, significance and religious meaning.

THEME

Choose a theme that has meaning for you. Think about adapting a theme from a recent holiday, like re-living the beauty of Tuscany or surrounding yourself in a tropical oasis. Keep the climate of your garden in mind, this will influence what plants will grow. In warm arid areas, choose a cactus garden or maybe a simple olive grove, while oriental gardens do well in a cooler climate. In wetter warm areas, plant a lush tropical garden — a tamed jungle that will appreciate the additional moisture, humidity and heat.

ABOVE: Handmade screens personalise this garden and add to its individuality. BELOW: Remember the subtlety of the seasons and the wonderful effects you can generate.

PERSONALISING YOUR PLACE

Personalise your place with sculpture, whimsy and found objects. A well-chosen sculpture, a piece of outdoor furniture or a feature pot will add to the ambience of your garden. This is a simple way of creating your own individual place. I like to include changeable installations in my garden for different events. An Arabian night can be jazzed up with removable fabric curtains that cascade around entertaining areas, while wrought iron candelabras quickly bestow a festive mood on an outdoor medieval feast. This transforms the garden into a stage, where the drama of life unfolds, as it should.

Have you ever been on holiday somewhere special and wanted to bring the atmosphere home? Bring back mementos and ornaments to place in your garden. There are no rules — you are creating a garden for your own spirit, no-one else's.

LEFT: *The fixed colour of the block walls match the transient colour of the flowers.* **MIDDLE & RIGHT:** *The iceplant (Sedum spectabilis) is a perennial that changes colour thoughout the seasons as shown here.*

SEASONS

The mood of your garden changes with the seasons. Some people design their gardens around such seasonal intricacies as the fine shadows of bare branches on feature walls. Maybe it's an overwhelming spring display of flowering trees that create colourful carpets as the petals fall. Perhaps the dream is to create a forest to house the cacophony of the cicadas' chorus at the height of summer.

COLOUR

Think of the garden as a work of art that depends on the combination of colours rather than the individual colour patches within it. Colour can be used with intensity or subtlety, and can basically be divided into hot and cool. Look at the colour wheel and decide on the palette that will suit your personality and home. Look first to your favourite colours and then place them against a colour wheel. Colours next to each other on the colour wheel are harmonious, colours opposite one another are dramatic and contrasting. Remember colour and the combinations of colours evoke certain moods and atmos-

phere. Paint colour swatches, which you can usually obtain from a hardware store, can be very helpful when playing with colour, tone and shade.

Fixed colour

Begin by selecting the fixed colours. Such colours remain the basic background to the garden. The colour of walls, the house, any fences and the ground surfaces will not change. They will inform the colour combinations in the rest of the garden.

Transient colour

Transient colours come and go, like the intense red foliage of deciduous trees in autumn or the yellow meadow of daffodils in spring or the white carpet of frangipani flowers in summer. Plantings, foliages and flowers will change with the seasons and provide transient colour combinations through the year. Research when things flower and plan for different colour combinations. Maybe you would like to have cool coloured flowers in summer to lessen the feel of heat, and conversely have warm colours in winter to heat things up.

putting your plan into action

If you are wondering where to go from here, look at my top 10 design secrets to get you started. By now you should know what functions you want to include — outdoor living room, clothesline, pond, secret place and focal point — and have a working site plan. Tape your bubbles onto a copy of the site plan to give you a clear indication of their final location. Work out the required size for each area. Use another site plan as an overlay to start your final design.

Start with your site plan that locates all the features you wish to retain. Overlay different design proposals with butter paper. Eventually a general design will emerge. Sometimes I find that the best design uses ideas from different proposals, so don't be afraid to combine them. Isolate design aspects to strengthen the design. Use a pencil so you can erase and change schemes. Use the planting symbols shown on this page for groundcovers, shrubs and trees. For a professional look to your plan, use different pen thicknesses for different garden layers, starting with the finest pen for the lowest groundcover level and thicker pens for overhead trees.

Look back over your list of desires, opportunities, constraints and garden images that have been listed and collected in your garden sketchbook. Are you on the right track? Take the plans outside and pace them out. Try to visualise what you have designed. If visualising the spaces is too tricky, mark out the design on the

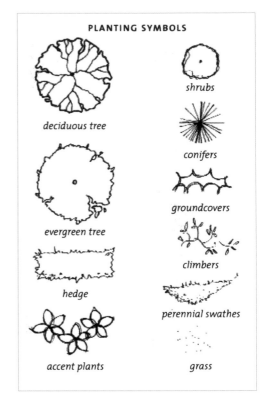

Have fun overlaying design ideas over your working design plan.

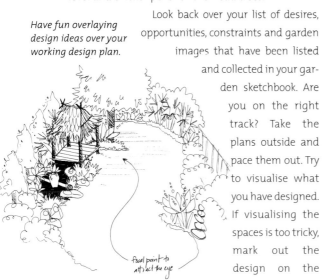

focal point to attract the eye

PLANTING SYMBOLS

deciduous tree

evergreen tree

hedge

accent plants

shrubs

conifers

groundcovers

climbers

perennial swathes

grass

ground with mark-out spray and you will be able to see the picture evolving.

let's start

Stage the construction and development of your garden. It is impossible to do all the work at once, and even if you could, it is essential to stagger the process to spread the workload and decide which features should be built first.

STAGE ONE

Complete any clearout and earthworks that need to be done. Remove weeds, salvage unwanted shrubs and trees. Stockpile any materials, such as pavers, bricks and rocks for reuse. Transplant any plants which need to be moved into their new location or store in pots if you must until they can go into their new home. Drainage and irrigation need to be addressed. Placement of water pipes for garden taps and electrical cables should be done now.

STAGE TWO

Give priority to essential features and large projects, such as driveways, paths, water features and garden buildings. Fences and garden walls need to be built to add privacy. Now mark out the design lines on the garden. Snake the hose around or mark the lines with a can of spray paint. Improving your soil and establishing the all-important compost heap is the next priority. This is also the time to order your plants from nurseries, and to start propagating from seeds or cuttings.

STAGE THREE

Finish off the hard work, like paving and garden edging. Plants can be planted out into nutritious soil and heavily mulched. Plant feature trees before climbers to give them a good head start. I like to leave the more fragile plants and the lawn to last as they are often ruined by pedestrian traffic.

STAGE FOUR

Finally, start adding sculptures, ornaments and smaller focal points, like pots and containers as funds permit. Garden furniture can now be added. This is the exciting stage. It is now that you can see the garden beginning to develop a personal flair, spirit and soul.

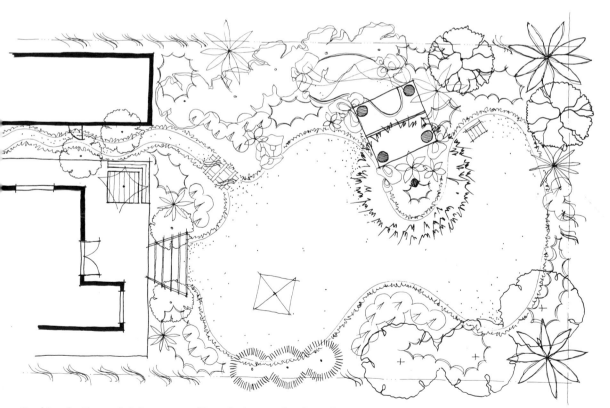

Combine planting symbols to come up with a 2-D planting plan that indicates texture, placement and size.

top ten design secrets

1. Keep it **simple**. Use only a limited range of materials and try to repeat colours, materials or shapes to create unity.

2. Blur the boundaries of the garden. Enclose the garden with climbers and hedges so the edges of the garden cannot be seen. This will increase the feel of the garden transforming it into an intimate urban oasis.

3. Create the illusion of **space** by:
- light coloured walls;
- small unit paving like cobblestones to trick the eye into thinking they are larger;
- a trompe l'oeil to deceive the eye into thinking the space continues;
- increasing the sense of perspective by adding a sculpture to end the vista.

4. Start with a bold **framework**. This will provide the structural backbone to the garden just like the walls of a house. The framework should include a bold design, strong layout and vibrant shapes. You can then add the elements of planting, sculpture and lighting to soften the overall effect.

5. Borrow pleasant scenery from any neighbouring property. Plan views of trees or structures, allowing these aspects to become part of your garden experience. This will provide a larger and fuller garden composition.

6. Add **water** in any way you can. It will liven things up by providing light and movement.

7. Textural surfaces. Add detail and decoration — pebbles, mosaics, stones, bagged masonry surfaces, recycled glass, mulch and reed fencing all contribute to the layering of textures within the garden. This layering of textures will give the garden richness.

8. Plan for **foliage colour** as well as flower colour to increase the tonal depth of your garden. Paths add intrigue, inviting exploration.

9. The best gardens are **multifaceted** and **multilayered**. Planting should have a variety of height levels, a succession of seasonal interest and a few surprises along the way.

10. Use a focal point to catch the eye. Attract attention to a particular vista. Limit yourself to one focal point per garden view.

inspire

bush

Paper daisies rustle in the breeze. Blue wrens and blue tongue lizards. Hiding . Happy. Never ending natter of larrikin lorrikeets. The warble of magpies. Skyward straining Gymea lilies and the soft velvet claws of kangaroo paws. The bush garden takes centre stage.

A bush garden is a wonderful way to show off your love of nature, showcase Australian plants and attract birds whilst providing a homely habitat for local fauna. The bush garden provides a canvas for self-expression and becomes an invaluable tool for self-education. We all fell in love with native plants back in the 1970s but soon became tired of the restricted plant palette available to us as home gardeners. But the good news is that sensational new cultivars and varieties are now available, performing better than ever in Australian home gardens and overseas.

the bush garden

You can create an Australian-only garden or mix exotics and natives together. Some exotic plants generate wonderful food for birds. Australian plants are tough and hardy but also provide outstanding displays of unusual flowers throughout the year. Winter is a quiet but beautiful time in the bush garden as there are so many plants that brighten up a cold winter's day. Australian gardens tend to require less care but still have a few basic requirements. Good free-draining soil is essential, with a pH of around 6. Light pruning will be necessary after flowering to keep shrubs compact and full. Feeding with a low-phosphate plant food in early spring and again in early summer is recommended.

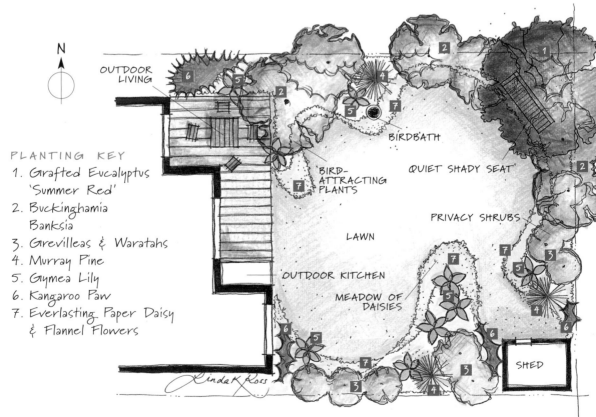

N

OUTDOOR LIVING

BIRDBATH

QUIET SHADY SEAT

BIRD-ATTRACTING PLANTS

PRIVACY SHRUBS

LAWN

OUTDOOR KITCHEN

MEADOW OF DAISIES

SHED

PLANTING KEY
1. Grafted Eucalyptus 'Summer Red'
2. Buckinghamia Banksia
3. Grevilleas & Waratahs
4. Murray Pine
5. Gymea Lily
6. Kangaroo Paw
7. Everlasting Paper Daisy & Flannel Flowers

Linda K Ross

GARDEN DESIGN PLAN

Sometimes a garden design comes together with just one simple curve. This is a family garden, so garden beds were resricted to the edges giving plenty of open space for the children to play, kick the ball around and rumble with the dog. Steer clear of straight lines, bush gardens suit rampant sweeping lines.

SUITABLE CLIMATE

There are Australian plants for every part of Australia, so select the ones suitable for your local area. Australian plant nurseries will be able to advise the best plants for your soil, climate and rainfall.

DESIGN TRICKS

Gardens for young families need to be designed differently. By making the lawn larger, bolder and simpler we have made it easier to mow. Simple timber benches are dotted around, making great viewing platforms for family bird watching.

PLANTING SCHEME

This family watches the birds from the back step. It's a clever way of getting children excited and interested in bird life and their ecology. Planting in layers creates an intimate garden, and boundary plantings of flowering shrubs screen unwanted views and attract birdlife. Plant a large mix of Australian plants to attract both honeyeaters and seedeaters to the garden and create an explosion of colour throughout the year. Beds of paper daisies and flannel flowers create floral sweeps. Spiky shrubs, such as grevilleas, banksias, yellow drumsticks and Australian fuchsia create a protected haven for the small birds. Taller trees provide enclosure.

RIGHT: *Maximize usable space by keeping planting around the boundaries. Island bed gardens are old fashioned and impractical when it comes to playing a family game of soccer.*

OPPOSITE: *Rainbow lorrikeets will be attracted to the flowers of the Queensland firewheel tree **(Stenocarpus sinuatus)*** **ABOVE:** *The creamy yellow drumstick flowers of the isopogon provide a protected habitat for finches.*

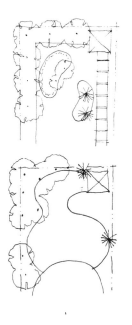

birds in the garden

Birds love a sanctuary where they feel safe to feed on nectar and seeds as well as find shelter and eventually breed. A supply of fresh water is very important as birds need to drink while feeding to aid the digestion of dry seeds. They also need water to bathe and splash in to maintain the condition of their feathers. A cat-proof birdbath should be placed up high on a pedestal and surrounded by spiky foliage in which the birds can take refuge and feel secure. Change the water regularly.

Plant a variety of flowering Australian plants to provide nectar, seeds and shelter throughout the entire year. Many natives do flower in winter. Don't be tempted to supplement the diet of the local birds' with mince or seed and nectar mixes. This makes them lazy and too reliant on you.

Keep cats inside the house at night and put two bells on their collars to prevent them hunting our native bird life. Create shelter and nesting places for your local birds by hanging bird boxes in the trees.

planting list

Attracting honeyeaters

All 69 species of honeyeaters have special brush-tipped tongues to collect honey from curved tubular flowers. Rainbow lorikeets bury their heads in banksias and bottlebrush. Try the following flowers high in nectar to attract honeyeaters:

▶ Australian fuchsia (*Correa* hybrids)
▶ Bottlebrush (*Callistemon* 'Dawson's River Weeper')
▶ *Crowea exalata* 'Bidelong Compact'
▶ Emu bush (*Eremophila nivea* 'Spring Mist')
▶ Grevillea (*Grevillea* 'Sandra Gordon', 'Pink Surprise', 'Moonlight', 'Sylvia')
▶ Heath banksia (*Banksia ericifolia*)
▶ Kangaroo paw (*Anigozanthus* hybrids)
▶ Wax flower (*Eriostemon myoporoides*)

Attracting seed eaters

Parrots, rosellas and cockatoos enjoy the seeds of wattles and conifers. Brightly coloured grass finches will visit to feed on grass seed and if there is shelter they may even make nests in the grass. The following plants will supply these local birds with the seed they need rather than supplying it artificially.

▶ Banksia 'Birthday Candles'
▶ Cycad (*Cycas revoluta*)
▶ Cypress pine (*Callitris columellaris*)
▶ Gymea lily (*Doryanthus excelsor*)
▶ Ivory curl tree (*Buckinghamia celsissima*)
▶ Pincushion bush (*Hakea laurina*)
▶ Wattle (*Acacia* spp.)

Attracting insect eaters

Moonlight on white and lemon flowers will attract moths and other insects during the night, providing food for many insect-eating birds. These include grevilleas 'Moonlight', 'Sandra Gordon', 'Honey Gem', 'Sylvia' and the ivory curl tree (*Buckinghamia*).

Grevillea 'Pink Surprise'

Grevillea 'Sandra Gordon'

Cycad

Heath banksia

Cycad seeds

Grevillea 'Moonlight'

plant profiles

 height & width of plant

 good for pot

 prefers full sun

 prefers partial shade

 tolerates full shade

 frost hardy

 frost tender

BELOW: *These velvet kangaroo paws are soft to touch.*

GRAFTED FLOWERING GUMS

Eucalyptus 'Summer Beauty', Summer Red',
Summer Snow', 'Brilliant Orange'

    5 m x 4 m

showy flowers attract birds

This small growing showy Australian native must be the best tree around. Bringing in the local birds and providing simply beautiful flowers all summer long. Great in a small courtyard, terrific as a street tree (growing below the wires). Huge heads of gum flowers with colours ranging from red, pink and white to mauve and orange. Ornamental gum nuts persist well after the flowers have faded.

> Select grafted gums if you live on the east coast of Australia. Feed with Osmocote for native plants. They do extremely well in harsh coastal windy positions.

KANGAROO PAW

Anigozanthos species

   varied heights
2 m x 1 m – 0.5m x 0.5m

bird-attracting velvet flowers

Renowned for its velvety kangaroo paws or 'claws', this accent plant impresses with its long flowering period. It comes in various colours including many of the warmer shades, bicolours and pinks. Look out for the hybrids as they flower more profusely and regularly. The green flowering form, 'Green Machine', is also tolerant of light frost.

> Need sandy soils and a warm position to grow best. Plants are very often attacked by ink spot disease (shown as black spots). Remove affected foliage and spray plant with Mancozeb Plus. Propagate new plants by root division in spring.
> Look out for the Bush Gem series — resistant to disease and more compact growers.

IVORY CURL TREE

Buckinghamia celsissima

     3 m x 3 m

good in large tubs

A real stunner, the ivory curl tree can be grown as a large shrub or a small tree. Originally from the rain-forests on the eastern seaboard, this large shrub is perfectly suited to the bush garden. The long exqui-site ivory spires rise like a creamy halo, timing themselves perfectly for Australia Day.

> The ivory curl tree needs well-drained soil in a sunny position.

LEFT: *Flowers are followed by huge gum nuts, great for floral decorations.* **TOP:** *Ivory curl tree.* **BOTTOM:** *Swan River daisies create a colourful carpet.*

SWAN RIVER DAISY

Brachycome multifida 'Break-o-day'

     0.3 m x 0.5 m

they like it hot

These make superb floral carpets, useful fillers for rock crevices and pretty in pots. They come in blue, mauve, white and lemon. They love the hot and dry weath-er, so don't overwater them.

> Extend flowering from to spring to autumn by trimming finished flowers.

plant profiles

WARATAH
Telopea speciosissima

     3 m x 1.2 m

red flower heads

The floral emblem for New South Wales is a majestic garden plant although it can be slightly temperamental. I've seen this beauty growing brilliantly in a range of conditions, so it is a good idea to persist. The scarlet crimson flower heads are borne in large domes which are carried high and proud by slightly straggly shrubs. Place in a sheltered spot away from strong winds.

> Prune lightly after flowering to keep compact. Keep the soil on the sandy side with low fertility. They are prone to root rot when grown in wet soils. Plant small to get the best results.

LEFT: *Waratah sits tall and proud.* **RIGHT:** *Paper daisies last forever, simply pick and hang upside down to dry.*

EVERLASTING DAISY
Bracteantha bracteata
(syn Helichrysum bracteatum)

    0.8 m x 0.4 m

great spring meadow

A lot of research has been done on Australia's beautiful array of paper daisies to make them suitable for the home garden. Look out for new forms of the everlasting daisy in your local nursery. We've chosen a gelato-coloured mix — lemon, white and gold — to plant in our garden. Everlasting daisies tend to self-seed throughout the garden.

look to nature for inspiration

The bush garden celebrates the detail in nature. Some native flowers are microscopic while other flowers like the waratah are so big and bright they seem to show off. And that's exactly what they are doing, showing their brilliance to attract pollinators and prolong their life. So at the end of a busy day you can sit back in your bush garden and admire the honeyeaters darting in and out and reflect on the fact that you have created something beautiful and in harmony with nature.

Look at your local environment for inspiration. If you live near the beach, plant a coastal garden with coastal banksias and coastal rosemary. If you live in a moist gully then go for a rainforest garden, full of ferns and native violets. If you live in a new housing development, select trees to give summer shade. Choose drought-tolerant Aussie plants to keep water usage and costs down.

GARDEN CARE

When creating a place for native wildlife use organic gardening methods and as few chemicals as possible.

Bush gardens tend to require less care, but they still need a few basic requirements. Here are a few tips.

Good quality free-draining soil with a pH of around 6 is essential. Be careful with what you use to feed your Australian plants, as they dislike fertiliser with high ratios of trace elements, such as potassium and phosphorus. Australian soils are ancient, leached and low in nutrient, too much fertiliser will burn the surface. Feed with well rotted manures, either cow, sheep or stable manures. Make up liquid manures by soaking in water and watering in. Lightly prune your natives after each flush of flowering to keep them compact and full. A light pair of hedge trimmers is perfect for pruning.

the potted bush garden
The colours of the Australian bush in a nutshell — a mixture of the best Australian wildflowers are planted in a half wine barrel. Select a potting mix designed for native plants — this will drain freely and contain beneficial micro-organisms to aid the growth of natives. Place the pot in a sunny, protected position and keep watered. We suggest:
- Kangaroo paw (*Anigozanthos* 'Bush Gem')
- Everlasting or straw daisy (*Bracteantha bracteantha*)
- Swan River daisy (*Brachycome multifida*)
- Waratah (*Telopea speciossimia*)
- Banksia 'Birthday Candles'
- Happy wanderer (*Hardenbergia violacea*)

create

Now comes the time for you to turn your thoughts, plans and designs into a reality. In this chapter we will look at making your dream come alive with some helpful advice.

Understanding the garden basics will save you time and minimise costly mistakes. If you get the basics right, like soil, watering, plant nutrition and plant selection, your garden will love you for it. My quick pest and disease guide will help you identify the other living things in your garden and show you how to prevent them from doing too much damage. A garden calendar reminds you when things need to be done. Lush healthy gardens, like the one above, are easy to achieve with minimum stress and maximum satisfaction.

top ten tips for a healthy garden

1. Love your soil! Improve it with animal manures, fallen leaves and your own compost. You are crazy if you don't improve the soil before you plant.

2. If you have dreadful soil, start by sowing a crop of **lupins, beans or peas**. They are green crops that improve soil nutrients. When the crop is mature dig it into the soil before planting four weeks later.

3. Want the best insurance policy for your garden in times of drought? Add **water crystals** to the soil before planting, especially under a new lawn.

4. You'll get the best results by **planting your garden in autumn**. The soils are warm and the air is cooling off.

5. **Plant small**. Buy tubestock and smaller sized pots, as smaller plants will establish themselves better and more quickly than larger plants.

6. **Seaweed** is caviar for gardens. Mulch it, spread it around and most of all spray it over the entire garden – leaves and roots. It strengthens your plants making them resistant to disease. Collect it yourself (check amounts with your local council) or buy it in the form of seaweed solution. Water in every month and especially on new plants and seedlings.

7. Plant **groundcovers** to **choke out weeds**. This will save you time weeding!

8. Want free fertiliser? **Wood ash** from the fireplace is useful as it contains potassium, great for encouraging fruit and flowers. **Rabbit droppings** are also high in nutrient but are best used within your compost.

9. Plant herbs like garlic, chives, rue, tansy and pyrethrum daisy through the garden. They look great, taste good but also repel many annoying insects from nibbling your plants.

10. Start a **compost heap** to recycle your kitchen waste — oh and by the way having two **chickens** is great — I speak from experience — they'll lay an egg a day as well as supply essential manures for the garden.

climate

Australia is a huge continent, approximately five per cent of the world's land surface, covering 7,682,300 square kilometres in area. It comprises many varying climatic zones, each affected by altitude, proximity to the sea or a large body of water, and geographical features, such as deserts or flat plains, mountains, valleys and plateaus. While some gardening books refer to nearly a dozen different climatic zones, and some books and magazines have taken to adapting their own version of climatic zones, much of this detailed information is irrelevant here. The important point to remember when designing your garden is that low temperature is the most limiting factor to plants. And that doesn't just mean snow. Frost and bitterly cold winds can be just as restricting to plant growth as a metre of snow.

MICROCLIMATE

Each individual garden has its own micro climate that may differ from the regional climatic pattern. List the highest and lowest temperature during summer and winter, the average number of frosts each winter (if any), wind velocity and the humidity. Create protected warmer sites by building walls and place frost sensitive plants under trees or in protected areas near the house. To help you, I have divided the Australia into five basic climatic zones.

TROPICAL

This zone is confined to the top of Queensland, Northern Territory and Western Australia. It has just two seasons, wet and dry. The wet season is from December to March and is when the cyclone threat is high. Summer has high rainfall, high temperatures in excess of 35°C and extreme humidity. Winter is

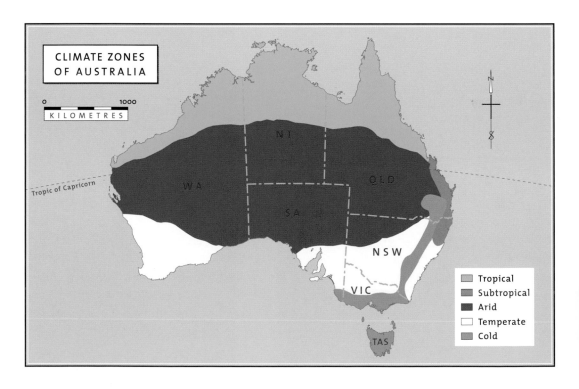

dry, has high temperatures but lower humidity. Tropical gardens explode out of the ground during the wet but are prone to fungal diseases due to the high rainfall.

Areas: Darwin, Townsville, Cairns, Broome.

ARID

Rainfall is erratic and variable, and less than 250 mm. Temperatures can exceed 40°C during the day and plunge to below 0°C at night. Spreads across Central Australia down to the Great Australian Bight.

Areas: Carnarvon, Kalgoorlie, Alice Springs, Longreach

SUBTROPICAL

Subtropical zones have high temperatures, medium humidity and are generally frost free. They have wet summers and dry winters. Generally less rainfall and lower winter temperatures than in the tropical zone.

Areas: Brisbane, Rockhampton to Coffs Harbour, Lismore, Grafton.

TEMPERATE

This temperate zone is a mild climatic zone with high summer temperatures and the possibility of inland frosts during the winter months. Rainfall is evenly distributed throughout the year.

Areas: Perth, Adelaide, Sydney, Newcastle, inland New South Wales.

COLD

The cold zone has frosts, the possibility of snow and sleet in winter. It has a relatively short summer growing season but it does have four distinct seasons. Rainfall is evenly spread but sometimes drier in summer in the southern reaches.

Areas: This colder zone follows the line of the Great Dividing Range to the Victorian border and includes all of Tasmania, Blue Mountains, Canberra, Orange, Goulburn, southern Victoria.

soil

Let's start from the beginning and have a good look at soil. Essential to plant health is soil that's rich, healthy and full of worms. As a garden designer and horticulturist, I see different garden soils every day. When I see plants struggling to survive in harsh soil that is baked hard on top, I nearly cry. Tears turn to shock when the client asks me why the garden isn't growing very well. I tell them the most important thing to remember is healthy soil will result in a healthy garden. If you have poor soil you must put extra effort in improving it. Put as much consideration into the soil as you do in plant selection.

The topsoil is where everything happens — most groundcovers, shrubs and perennials use the top 40 cm of soil. Topsoil is usually full of goodies that come

TOP: *Your soil should be good enough to eat. Feed the soil and not the plants. Make your own composted soil at home.*

from fallen leaves and decayed organic matter. You need to increase the quality and depth of this soil for your garden to really shine. Topsoil is very precious. Australia is an ancient landmass and the topsoil has been greatly eroded over time. In some parts of Australia the loss of topsoil amounts to 200 tonnes per hectare annually. In the domestic situation, topsoil should never be removed or buried when building. If a building project is planned, remove your topsoil first and stockpile it for use later in garden beds and lawn areas. In fact we have worked for the last 30 years by the 'topsoil' mantra that it is far better to 'improve than import'. Unfortunately, in housing estates many new gardens are established on less than desirable soil.

Whilst I have bought bagged soil conditioners from nurseries, I make most of my own soil-improving compost by combining garden straw, cow manure, horse manure, chicken manure, prunings, grass clippings and kitchen scraps. More information on composting can be found on page 118. Initially, just place these materials in layers on a heap and allow them to rot down. After five weeks or so, this decomposing organic matter is ready to be incorporated into your garden beds. Compost will improve the soil dramatically and attract your garden's little helpers, the worms. Worms make long tunnels deep into the earth, which allow air and water to penetrate deep down, improving the soil texture and making it easier to cultivate.

The added organic material improves the texture of the soil and also greatly aids the retention of moisture and nutrients, thus enabling easier penetration by roots and quicker plant establishment. This simple and inexpensive method of soil conditioning is equally important and beneficial to sandy soils as it is to earth of clay origins.

Garden soil should be well aerated and not compacted — these air pockets retain moisture essential to plant growth. Your soil should also be well drained and not boggy. Plant roots need air and moisture to grow, otherwise they will in effect drown. Your soil should be deep enough to support good root growth. Bulbs, annuals, vegetables and perennials require about 30 to 40 centimetres of soil; shrubs require a minimum of 50 to 70 centimetres and trees need several metres to grow into mature specimens. Soil that is loose, friable and organic will be able to absorb all the nutrients needed by your plants. This has to be the best insurance policy you could get for your garden. Good soil is called loam; it is a balance of clay, silt, sand particles and organic matter.

SOIL TEST

Determining the exact type of soil in your garden is a scientific process. Soil laboratories can provide a complete soil analysis, but for you independent types here is an easy test. Collect half a cupful of soil, add a little water and mix until lump free. Drain the excess moisture and squeeze the soil into a ball in the palm of your hand. The rough guide is:

- **Loamy sand** — the sample will be sandy and just holds.
- **Sandy loam** — the sample holds but falls apart easily if touched and gritty sand grains can be felt when rubbed between the thumb and forefinger.
- **Loam** — the sample mass holds its shape but can break apart like plasticine.
- **Clay** — the sample mass holds its shape and is very hard, sticky and elastic. It is fine and smooth textured.

SOIL PH

Much is made of knowing your soil pH, to the point of confusion. It should be stated that many gardeners achieve great success without ever knowing the pH of their soil. On the other hand, once the pH is determined it will not be necessary to check your soil

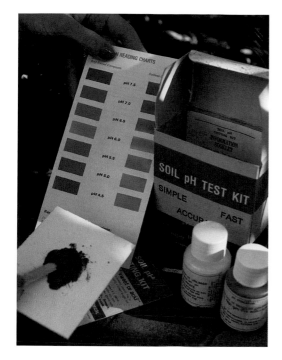

ABOVE: *Keen to experiment? Start by determining the pH of your garden soil.*

again other than to confirm the reading after any attempt to change any over-acidity or over-alkalinity. Technically, the pH of the soil is integral to the health of your garden and comes down to the ratio of acid to alkaline elements, or more simply, the percentage of lime in the soil. The pH of soil is measured on a scale of 1 to 14, with 1 being extremely acid and 14 extremely alkaline. The majority of garden plants will enjoy neutral soils of about 7, so you should aim for a range between 5.5 and 7.5 in your garden. A pH of 6.5 allows all the plant nutrients to be available to the plants quickly and easily.

There are some exceptions to the rule. Plants such as azaleas, ericas, camellias, gardenias, rhododendrons are acid lovers and can be somewhat temperamental. These plants prefer a stronger acid-based soil of pH 5.0 to 5.5. Plants such as magnolias, orchids, the majority of bulbs, native plants and ferns prefer just a slightly acid soil of pH 5.5 to 6.0. If your soil is too acidic you can add lime, agricultural lime or dolomite. Alkaline soils are harder to correct.

Regular additions of compost will help in the long term to increase the acidity of your garden soil. Small applications of aluminium sulphate or iron sulphate (2 tablespoons per metre) or sulphur (4 tablespoons per square metre) will also help reduce alkalinity.

PREPARING YOUR SOIL

If you enjoy making soil healthy you will be a gardener for life. Soil preparation is hard work and involves getting dirty. Basically, add as much organic matter to your garden as you can get your hands on. Use any type of manure — sheep, cow, horse or chicken. Manure will gently improve the nutrient level of the soil as will spent mushroom compost, decomposed leaves and vermicompost (worm castings).

Here is a basic guide for inexpensive soil preparation:

▶ **Turn your soil** with a garden fork or a mattock, to aerate the top 40 cm of the soil.

▶ Cover the soil liberally with **manure**. It can be fresh, but well rotted is preferable.

▶ Sprinkle **blood and bone** at the rate of one handful per square metre.

▶ Cover the area with a thick blanket of **mulch** (sugar cane, tea-tree, lucerne hay, garden straw or compost).

▶ Wait 10 weeks and then **dig in**, incorporating all the ingredients into your soil. Avoid the use of any chemical insecticides as these will harm the hard-working earthworms. By now your soil will have improved out of sight and is ready for you to get planting.

Double-digging

If you are starting from scratch, the best piece of advice I can give is to double dig. This means digging the soil out to a spade's depth then turning over another spade's depth and adding the original soil with extra organic matter or compost back to the garden. Sounds like a lot of work? It is, but it's also worth the effort. You'll find the plants will never look back and will explode into growth and billowing flower displays.

Leaves are free ... so use them

Spent autumn leaves in the form of leaf mould are one of the best soil conditioners. Leaves are free, recyclable and easy to use. Simply rake up autumn leaves and place them in bags or in a pile, sprinkling layers with a little blood and bone as you go. Let the leaves break down, turning the heap weekly with a garden fork. After four months, spread them in a 7- to 10-cm layer over your garden. If you want to give your compost a head start, running the lawnmower over the leaves first to shred them will reduce the time it takes for them to decompose. After adding the leaf mould to the garden, let the earthworms do the hard work for you. They will ingest the decomposed leaves and take them deep down into the soil. Their excreta will enrich your soil and their tunnels will aerate it. (Note that fallen gum leaves also make useful compost but are best combined with other organic matter.)

IMPORTING TOPSOIL

If you don't have any soil to start with or if you are in a huge rush, you will need to import topsoil. If the latter applies then here's a big tip. At some stage in your gardening experiences you will have to learn patience. Importing topsoil will give great short-term results, but it takes time to improve soil properly — it just doesn't happen overnight. Imported topsoil can have its own inherent problems. The presence of weed seeds within the soil is probably the worst risk. Remove any weeds as soon as you notice them. Chemically treat weeds such as oxalis and onion weed with glyphosate as these will quickly become a long-term nuisance. It is best to thoroughly incorporate the imported soil with your existing soil, as it will improve your own soil's fertility and structure.

Soils can also be improved with soil conditioner, such as Biogrow, which can be purchased at your local nursery. Using soil conditioners is more expensive than making your own compost but they do a similar job without the wait. Depending on your soil's fertility use one 30-kilogram bag per square metre. Some brands of soil conditioners have added granular wetting agents, water storage crystals and controlled release fertilisers.

> Remember when ordering soil from your landscape supplier that you are working on the long-term foundation of your garden and there is no substitute for quality.

PREPARATION OF CLAY SOILS

Hard and compacted clay soils are common in Australia. You might be pleased to learn that clay soils make a great base for your garden. The only problem with clay is that many of the nutrients are locked up within the clay particles, making them unavailable to the plants. If you have clay soils, use gypsum, liquid Groundbreaker or Clay Breaker, or organic matter to start breaking up the soil's structure to release the nutrients. Gypsum is simply sprinkled on while the liquid 'breakers' are connected to a hose and hosed in. This will work within weeks and save you long hours of digging with a spade. Most products designed to 'break up' clay require several applications over one year. By adding organic matter you will build up the height of your garden beds, supply plants with the right nutrients and increase drainage so they don't get wet feet.

PREPARATION OF SANDY SOIL

The problem with sandy soils is they have excessive drainage, so effective that all the nutrients and organic matter are leached out of the soil with rainfall and watering. The addition of compost or any organic matter will assist in retaining moisture and essential plant nutrients in the soil but will need to be continually replenished. The process of mulching, adding compost, even using organic fertilisers, needs to be repeated every three months. Don't lose heart, you will eventually win.

PREPARATION OF SILTY SOILS

Silty soils are usually high in nutrients and fertility but retain plenty of moisture and can become compacted easily. It is important to continually aerate the soil with a garden fork to lighten the soil and increase the air pockets within it. Add a mulch of fallen leaves and let the earthworms take them deep down. Don't work the soil while it's wet, it only encourages the clay to become more compact, let it dry out first.

the role of soil

IN PLANT GROWTH

Plants need a balance of different elements for growth. They obtain the basic elements of carbon, hydrogen and oxygen from water and air, but this is just the beginning. They also need another twelve essential elements for growth, flowering and fruiting. Gardeners can supply all these elements through organic matter, such as manures, inorganic and organic fertilisers and trace elements. The major elements of nitrogen, phosphorus and potassium are required in large amounts, while the minor elements, such as calcium, magnesium and sulphur, are needed in smaller quantities. A wide range of other elements is also required, albeit in even smaller amounts. These include boron, iron, copper and manganese. It is important to understand that while trace elements are significant to health, their deficiency is rarely a problem in gardens.

Trace elements act as catalysts, assisting plants to build compounds in the plant cells to utilise the major and minor elements present. The only time trace elements will need to be added is when there is an obvious deficiency. For example, lemons can show a grey 'stain' in the fruit that in some soils will be a sign of boron deficiency. Applying borax at the rate of 1 tablespoon dissolved in 8 litres of water around the dripline will fix the problem. An understanding of essential elements is important for plant growth but an excessive use of trace elements can cause toxicity in the soil. This is why complete fertilisers, such as Garden Gold, Gro Plus, and Osmocote, contain the main elements and the trace elements in carefully balanced quantities. Some fertilisers also contain wetting agents, which aid in getting the food down to the roots of the plant.

BELOW: *Citrus often get iron and magnesium trace element deficiency, shown by gradual yellowing of the leaves.*

115

compost

Each Australian household throws away almost a tonne of waste each year. Thirty-nine per cent of this could be easily composted and is pefect garden food!

Beware: composting can become an obsession! Always focus on the end result; the production of a material that will improve soil texture and manageability, retain nutrients, produce healthy plants and reduce run-off and soil erosion in your garden. Along the way you'll have fun, get some exercise and protect the environment. Every good gardener has at least one compost heap, and once you have seen the benefits you will want more. The returns are fourfold:

▶ By composting your household waste you reduce landfill.

LEFT: *No space for a heap? Use a compost bin.*
BELOW: *Since 1991 householders have doubled their recycling, but there is still a long way to go.*

▶ You will improve your garden soil organically and safely.
▶ Composting encourages beneficial earthworms, which means healthy soil, healthy shrubs, flowers and vegetables.
▶ Home-grown compost is free.

A simple formula for composting
• Start by pegging out a 2-metre square in a warm dry patch of the garden.
• Spread a thick layer of cow, horse and or chicken manure over the area plus a sprinkling of blood and bone. Pelleted manure is a good substitute for this.
• Add a layer of your kitchen waste. Use all your fruit and vegetable matter, eggshells, tea and coffee grounds and spent cut flowers. (Do not add meat or processed foods.)
• Add alternate layers of lawn clippings, garden prunings and even leafy weeds. (Do not add weeds with seed heads or bulbs. Seldom does the heat generated in the heap kill weed seeds.)
If you are impatient for results add additional layers of straw or lucerne.
• Fork over the pile weekly to ensure everything is mixed in well and if it hasn't rained, give it a sprinkle with the hose. The pile should be quite moist. Cover the pile in heavy rain, as you don't want the nutrients leaching out of the heap.

• After six to eight weeks you shouldn't be able to recognise anything in the pile. This indicates the compost is ready to use.
I should point out that this simple heaped method is slow but reasonably effective. The minute you stack the heap vertically in a wire cage or timber frame, the effectiveness increases dramatically.

worms

Worms are nature's little helpers. If you don't have room for a compost heap try a worm farm. Worm castings contain high levels of nitrogen, phosphorus and potassium and plenty of minor elements. Both earthworms and composting worms are important as they recycle nutrients into the soil. Worms increase the aeration of the soil, which increases the population of beneficial organisms in the soil and improves root growth. Organic gardeners are wild about worms as they help to create sustainable ecosystems.

A worm farm is a great alternative for people living in apartments, terraces and townhouses. These little guys make recycling kitchen waste easy by digesting half their own weight each day. Councils have well priced worm farms available, as they believe they cut back on landfill waste. Worm bins can be constructed from anything — wooden boxes or crates, old baths, laundry tubs, washing machine bowls, small water tanks and clean empty drums would all be perfect Drill a drainage hole in the bottom and put a drip tray underneath. Place several layers of newspaper bedding in the bottom and dampen. Top up with 15 cm of homemade compost or rich soil and cover with lucerne hay. Locate your worm farm in a semi-shaded and sheltered position. The best worm bedding is a 50:50 mix of manure and straw and should be changed once a year.

Worms love to eat food that is high in nitrogen, such as kitchen waste, grass clippings and even weeds, bread, leaves, straw and animal manure. Chop up your kitchen scraps or put them through a food processor, then add them to the farm in thin layers. A removable cover will regulate the moisture levels of the farm, which should be kept just moist but not saturated. Reduce evaporation and provide darkness by placing a damp hessian bag over the surface. An old piece of carpet is ideal. Be wary of the pH of your worm farm. If your worms are looking sluggish and have a reduced appetite, the farm may have become too acidic. Add a sprinkle of lime to correct the situation. Every time you add food, replace the damp hessian or newspaper. You'll know the worms are ready for more food if when you lift the cover they are wiggling madly on the surface.

Worms dislike centipedes, mites, birds, rats and ants, so try to keep these things away. Fertilisers, weedkillers or herbicides, pesticides, all chemicals generally, are bad news for worms. To avoid introducing pesticide sprays into the worms' food chain, where possible use garlic or rhubarb sprays to control insects in the garden and encourage such predatory creatures as ladybirds and mantids. Also, try to keep citrus peel and onion down to a minimum.

Composting worms that you buy from a nursery won't usually survive out in the garden — they will need their own worm farm. Purchase red worms or tiger worms also known as the manure worm, from a good nursery. One thousand worms cost around $10. Reduce their numbers every few years by giving them away to friends.

> Dilute the drip tray contents of your worm farm as homemade liquid manure feeds the entire garden at the rate of 1 part worm wee to 10 parts water.

watering wisely

Water wisely to maximise the amount of water available. Drought proof your garden with these simple water wise gardening tips.

▶ Mulch your entire garden thickly to retain moisture. Add the mulch to a moist garden. I always apply mulch just after rain. Make your own mulch by adding fallen leaves and your own compost.

▶ Add a simple efficient and well designed automatic watering system. Look at drip or micro-irrigation systems attached to tap timers. Water late in the day, or early in the morning.

▶ Water by hand as you will use less water this way than by using a sprinkler system. In summer give the garden a deep soak once a week.

▶ Choose waterwise plants that cope with hot conditions. Spotting plants with low water needs is easy, look for hairy leaves, small leaves, tough surfaces, silver reflective leaves or deep roots.

▶ Think about recycling greywater. This will take commitment and planning. Hoses that bring greywater outside (that is water from the bath, shower and laundry) can be connected to a surge tank. A subsoil irrigation system can deliver this water directly into the soil. There are health issues as regards to pooling of surface greywater, so avoid it on vegetable or food plants.

▶ Don't waste those first few litres before hopping into the shower. Collect the water in a bucket and use it to water your indoor plants.

▶ Water-saving products, such as Rainsaver crystals, swell up when wet and hold the water for the roots to seek out, which allows extra time between watering. They last up to six years.

▶ Cover your pool to reduce evaporation. This saves up to 30,000 L per pool per year.

▶ Group plants with similar water requirements together. Plant arid-loving plants on dry, high spots and consider bog plants that tolerate wet feet in low-lying area.

▶ The most effective way to water small pots is to dunk them in a bucket of water. Hold the pot under the surface until all the bubbles stop. The soil is now thoroughly wet. Mulch pots with pebbles.

▶ Research shows that gardeners use over 50 per cent of water on their lawns, so, to conserve water, consider reducing your lawn area and replacing it with gravel, drought-tolerant groundcovers, decking or paving. Leave your grass to grow longer than usual as longer grass has deeper roots therefore needs to be watered less.

▶ Watering the garden accounts for 36% of home water use. Save your good drinking water by installing a rainwater tank.

▶ Rainwater tanks are simple to install and will reduce your water bill. Most councils will allow rainwater tanks for garden use only. A 2250-L tank should be sufficient and cost around $1000. Buy a pump (possibly solar powered) so you can use this water for a drip irrigation system.

▶ Weeds compete with other plants for available water so keep your garden weed free by mulching thickly.

WETTING AGENTS

Water storage crystals will help conserve moisture in the soil. Add a teaspoon in the hole at planting time and use them in containers when potting up. When the soil becomes dry, it shrinks and water tends to run off rather than soak in. A wetting agent will prevent this from happening, particularly to sandy soils. Look out for products like Eziwet, Saturaid and Wettasoil.

> Water crystals last up to six years in the soil and are the gardener's insurance against dry spells.

mulch

Mulch, mulch, mulch — mulching is another insurance policy for your garden. If you mulch thickly and correctly your garden will be protected on the hottest days. Mulching deters weed growth, prevents soil erosion, conserves soil moisture, increases beneficial soil organisms, builds good soil structure and corrects poor gardening practices from the past. Mulch can be used to start a garden or to finish one off. Keep topping up your mulch each year, as it will gradually decompose adding nutrients to the soil. Keep mulch away from the stems of your plants as this will build up and increase the temperature around the trunk, leading to stem weakness and collar rot. There are many types of mulch on the market; some of the most effective are sugar cane, lucerne hay, tea-tree, bush chip and pine bark.

SUGAR CANE

This mulch is a by-product of the sugar industry and consists of the tops and leaves cut from sugarcane plants. The mulch is widely available and comes in a compressed bale. Sugar cane is perfect for cottage, rose and vegetable gardens.

LUCERNE HAY

This fabulous mulch contains high levels of carbon and nitrogen that it puts back into the soil. Add it to the compost to accelerate the decomposition process. Roses love the extra nutrients from lucerne. Some years ago a farming family near Forbes, in rural New South Wales, researched the varying qualities of lucerne available to farmers. This resulted in a premium quality product called Earth Cubes being released through nurseries. Only 100 per cent, superior quality first-cut lucerne is used in this product. It resembles biscuit-shaped breakfast cereal and will disintegrate when watered.

STRAW

Garden straw provides a great barrier for weeds. It is available in compressed bales from agricultural supply yards and nurseries. Use it to prop up strawberries and around citrus. Be aware that seeds from its origins may germinate in your garden.

PEA STRAW

Pea straw breaks down easily. Because it is a legume it can increase soil fertility as well as being an ideal mulch. Be wary of pea germination coming up through the mulch. Weed out young seedlings as they appear.

TOP: *Garden straw is a valuable way of conserving soil moisture and keeping weeds in check.*

LEFT TO RIGHT: *Garden straw props up newly planted seedlings increasing success. Gravel can be used as garden mulch and on pathways. Use your own compost to mulch new seedlings to give them the vital nutrients they need.*

TEA-TREE MULCH

Tea-tree mulch is the by-product of the tea-tree essential oil industry. Its dark colour provides a perfect foil and backdrop to plants in any garden, especially in subtropical and tropical gardens..

LEAF MULCH

Fallen leaves do a great job in retaining soil moisture, they are free and they look great in Australian bush gardens. To assist leaves to break down more quickly, mow over them on the lawn with a grass catcher and then place them on the garden.

PINE BARK

A waste product from the timber industry, containing bark from the radiata pine, red gum and blackbutt trees. Pine bark became very popular in the 1970s. Be careful to use bark chips that have had any growth-retarding resins leached out. Leaving the mulch out in the rain for several weeks will do this. Add a handful of urea to combat the nitrogen drawdown affect. Coloured pine bark is now available dyed with red, yellow, black, green and blue vegetable dyes.

PEBBLES AND GRAVELS

Pebbles and gravels are often used to give an interesting effect. The gravel garden has become a garden style with the entire garden being mulched in pea-sized pebbles. Colours range from gold, white, brown, black, green, cream and sandstone.

SEAWEED MULCH

Where councils and authorities permit, collect seaweed from the beach. Seaweed contains nutrients that aid plant growth, strengthen cell walls and encourage resistance to pests and disease. Wash the seaweed of salt, leave to dry, shred, soak to make a gel and dilute one part to ten parts water, then spray.

nutrition

INORGANIC FERTILISERS

The analysis of fertilisers is expressed as a percentage of the nitrogen, phosphorus and potassium they contain, which is then listed as a ratio of N:P:K on the side of the packet. For example, N:P:K, 10.5:2.5:8.5. NPK fertilisers come in powder, granular and water-soluble forms, and straight liquids. Controlled release fertilisers such as Nutricote and Osmocote are pelleted or coated with a waxy or polymer resin material and are released depending on soil temperature and water penetrating the granule. One fertiliser, Triabon, has no coating but has a quick-release characteristic and then a slow-release organic release process. Many commercial nurseries use this fertiliser with considerable success. Packaged as Garden Gold, it is available for home gardeners with the benefit of an added granular wetting agent. Another advantage of this advanced fertiliser is that it contains trace elements.

We feed with Magic Mulch: a family recipe made up of:
• 1 ice cream containers of pelleted manure
• 2 handfuls of a wetting agent
• 1 handful of a slow release fertiliser
Yum!

ORGANIC FERTILISERS
Manures

Where would we be without manure, nature's free fertiliser? Fresh manure cannot be used straightaway as it burns the fine hairy roots on plants, especially shallow roots, so leave fresh manure in a pile for 10 weeks to rot, or combine the manure as layers on your compost pile, watering it occasionally to aid the decomposition process. Animal manure contains the most important elements, nitrogen, phosphorus and potassium, but in lower concentrations than packaged fertilisers. The quantity of the elements fluctuates with the type of animal, their diet, and the amount of straw included in the manure. When you repeatedly add manure in large quantities a nitrogen deficiency will result, which you will need to correct by adding some extra nitrogen. This can easily be achieved by spreading around a little urea. Urea releases nitrogen into the soil within weeks, while the other nutrients break down slowly over the months. Urea is available in powdered form from the local nursery or garden hardware store and should be applied one handful every metre square. Water in thoroughly.

If you don't have access to fresh manures you may need to look further afield or buy it from a nursery. Wherever you get it from, manure makes delicious soil. Well-rotted manure can be combined directly into existing soil, used to mulch plants and added to compost.

Pellets, powders and liquids

Organic fertilisers have been popular with gardeners for decades. They are generally by-products of abattoirs or the food processing industry and include blood and bone, bonemeal and fishmeal. Their slow release of

More than just an egg a day
Liquid manure provides a vital but gentle organic feed. We make liquid feed from our chook manure. Use a hessian bag to suspend any animal manure in a large drum or bin filled with water. Leave for a week and then use the brew at the rate of one part liquid to three parts water. Refill the drum and repeat the process until the brew is too weak to use. Chooks are great as they eat snails, slugs, curl grubs as well as scoff all our kitchen waste.

nutrients is mainly dependent on soil organisms already present in the soil, so it may take several weeks before their nutrients are available to plants. Organic fertilisers don't contain any potassium.

In recent years the popularity of pelleted manures has risen dramatically. Dynamic Lifter is primarily chicken manure in a convenient pellet form. Organic Life, another brand of pellets, contains blood and bone, fishmeal, seaweed, composted organic matter and micro-organisms to stimulate soil.

Organic liquid conditioners have been available for years. Those derived from seaweed have always been considered soil and plant friendly. Maxicrop would be the best known and is made from imported kelp. Seasol is the other well-known brand and is made from local seaweed. Liquid seaweed has the added benefit of assisting new plants to become established and reduce transplant stress. Powerfeed comes from the makers of Seasol and includes fish and liquid composts. Nitrosol is boosted with liquid blood and bone. Carp fish from Australian rivers are processed into a valuable organic liquid fertiliser called Charlie Carp. Generally speaking, organic fertilisers, while being slowly available to plants, are gentle on them, easy to apply and less polluting of the environment.

BELOW: *The range of seaweed products on the market.*

plant selection

The best advice I can give you on how to choose a good plant is to walk around your neighbourhood and talk to other gardeners. The best thing about gardeners is that they are the friendliest and most generous people on earth. Soon you'll find yourself loaded with cuttings and seeds — a veritable botanic garden of plant material. Observe the plants that are growing successfully in your neighbourhood. Photograph your favourites. Take the photos to your local garden centre and ask a horticulturist to identify the plants.

Spend time deciding what plants will be best for your garden. List the requirements of your garden design and find plants that fit them. Before buying a plant, look it up in a general plant encyclopaedia to check if it will become a weed, if it will fit the allocated space once it matures, and its preferred climate and soil type. This way you will make the most of your purchases and won't make one of the most common mistakes of the novice gardener, the impulse buy.

Purchase your plants from a garden centre or use the many mail-order companies across Australia (see the Appendix on page 152). Filling your garden with plants from the local nursery can be expensive, so it's a good idea to buy only the essential plants for your landscape and then grow the rest from cuttings or seeds. Propagating your own plants keeps the cost down and you always get more plants than you bargained for. It's also fun. Some plants have Plant Breeder's Rights (PBR) or plant patents and can only be propagated for yourself and friends, not for sale. Join local and interstate garden clubs and specialist societies and seed clubs to take advantage of seed exchange schemes — you'll find some unusual varieties. Buying small plant plugs (struck cuttings and seedlings in small cells) through mail order companies can be a cheap way of obtaining plants.

TIPS TO CHOOSING WISELY

Here are some tips on what to look for when buying plants from a nursery, and what to avoid.

Bulbs

▶ Choose fresh, firm plump bulbs as soon as they're available in the season.

▶ Avoid any bulbs that are soft, mushy, discoloured or smell of mould or disease.

▶ Choose the largest bulbs as they will generally produce strong and healthy flowers.

▶ Ensure the bulbs have retained their papery outer covering as this protects them from damage.

▶ Mail order bulbs offer a bigger range, the latest varieties and early delivery of the best quality.

Shrubs

▶ Buy shrubs in smaller and cheaper pot sizes.

▶ Upturn the pot to check for circling or girdling roots. Girdling roots will strangle the plant.

▶ Inspect that all leaf growth is clean, healthy and free of disease and insect attack. Mealy bug is, unfortunately, a common pest of nursery stock and should be avoided wherever possible. It appears as 'cottonwool' on the roots.

▶ Do not buy the shrub if it has sparse twiggy growth or signs of repeated pruning and regrowth. Small, undersized flowers can also be a sign of poor growth.

Perennials

▶ Save money, buy the smaller and cheaper 100 mm pots. The plants will establish themselves more quickly.

▶ When you buy and plant in autumn, the roots have more time to establish themselves, making a stronger plant for spring.

▶ Do not buy a plant that has too many roots protruding though the pot.

ABOVE: *Save money by buying loose bulbs in bulk from bulb mail order companies. See list in the Appendix.*

▶ Check that bare-rooted plants have healthy roots, buds and leaves to avoid introducing disease into your garden.

▶ Check that the containers are free of moss and weeds, a clear indication that they have been cared for and are sun-hardened.

▶ Look for plants with several strong shoots or ones that are multi-planted in the pot so you can divide the clump before planting.

▶ Take the plant out of its pot and check that it has a well-established system of fine white roots that form a good root ball without being pot-bound.

Perennials, soft-wooded and herbaceous, are flowering and leafy plants whose roots remain alive from year to year. The tops often die down and are removed after flowering. Perennials grow, flower and multiply quickly. They develop into large clumps that can be divided usually in autumn. Examples include day lilies, sedums, agapanthus, coneflowers, dahlias, yarrow and penstemon. Perennials are useful for creating colour and an impact quickly.

CLOCKWISE FROM TOP LEFT:
Mass plant bulbs to give a bold effect.
▶ *Pick up a bargain in the 100-mm perennial section of your local nursery.* ▶ *Choose hedge plants with low branching laterals.*
▶ *Roses lining up for mail-order deliveries. Get them planted as soon as they arrive.*
▶ *Buy autumn foliage plants in autumn, so you know what colour they turn.* ▶ *Pre-order bare-rooted roses from mail-order rose nurseries to get the pick of the bunch.*
▶ *Bare-rooted roses look like sticks when sold in mid-winter, but they soon burst into leaf in spring.*

Hedges

▶ Choose hedging plants with strong bushy lateral growth low down on the plant as this will quickly form a denser hedge.

▶ Select healthy plants using the same criteria as for shrubs, and with visible new growth buds.

Roses

▶ Bare-rooted roses are best but they are becoming harder to find. Preferably, buy roses when dormant in the winter season. It is very hard to kill a dormant rose.

▶ Look out for a network of three to five strong stems no smaller than 1.0 to 1.2 cm in diameter and showing minimal thorn scars.

▶ Do not buy if there is evidence of dieback on any of the stems or black spots on the leaves.

▶ Check that the plants have a strong root framework.

▶ If buying potted roses during the year, choose young plants in small pots. Avoid plants that have been repotted several times and appear too big for the pot.

Deciduous trees

▶ Buy bare-rooted trees and shrubs in winter, ensuring the root framework is well developed and not dried out or damaged.

▶ Choose a tree with a strong straight stem and intact leading shoot. It's important for a feature tree to have a singular leader.

▶ If bare of leaves, check with the nursery staff that it is correctly labelled.

▶ Like bare-rooted roses, the root system won't be extensive but should have four or five thick established roots with clean pruning cuts from the digging and lifting process. This is very important and should be done on purchase to avoid introducing diseases into your garden.

pests and diseases

Allow me to share a secret. You don't need garden chemicals to be a gardener. Few traditional authors refer to this and I'm not sure why. Some older gardeners may even question my comments as being ignorant, possibly some people will start calling me a greenie and a radical. But for many years I have been experimenting with two gardens. One garden is a large tropical landscape with a vegetable patch and hundreds of potted succulents, ferns and bromeliads. The other garden, nearly as big, is a combination of traditional rose gardens, climbers, perennials, bulbs and seasonal displays of flowers and shrubs, also with a large vegetable plot and several enclosed garden rooms. The former garden has had no chemicals used on it and the latter has had only 'safe' organic-based chemicals used on a very limited basis. Organic products are often referred to in the media as being chemical free, but in all honesty, they aren't. It is just that they contain a vastly safer group of chemicals with natural origins.

BELOW: *This bug does no damage at all. It's just attracted to the petals of this 'Altissimo' rose.*

How is this, I hear you ask? Well, it's pretty easy. I think of my gardens like I think about myself. If I take care of myself, enjoy a balanced nutritious diet, take vitamins and obtain minerals through fresh fruit and vegetables, I remain strong, healthy and able to ward off colds, flu and disease. If I do the same to my garden, feed the soil with organic manures and minerals, and water the foliages with a seaweed solution, my garden becomes strong, healthy and able to resist disease, even insect attack. I do sometimes get the odd hungry caterpillar, but a garden is a living and balanced ecosystem with beneficial insects as well as the nastier ones. Using harmful sprays kills the good, the bad, the ugly and indifferent. They can also do damage to pets and local wildlife.

ECOLOGICAL BALANCE

Know your chemical and your pest — become educated about what it is you are using. You need to know the insect and its life cycle or your methods may not be effective. For instance evidence of borer activity does not necessarily mean they are still there. You should also learn how a chemical may affect other organisms as well as the target pest.

If you do use chemicals, select the most specific measure (for instance inject rather than spray; choose one that kills only that particular pest; apply herbicide directly to plant stems) and apply only at the specified rate.

It is better to live with a few spots, weeds or bugs; individual plants are not necessarily precious and do not have to be absolutely perfect. Even fruit and vegetables are still edible with blemishes. Recognise those insects that are beneficial, for example, those that prey on others such as certain ladybirds, and remember ants are nature's garbage collectors.

Weeds are not necessarily a problem either unless there is a real infestation or there is direct

LEFT: *Here are eggs from the beneficial lacewing, these will hatch and keep other insects in check.* **RIGHT:** *Ladybird larvae love eating aphids, so encourage them by reducing chemical sprays.*

competition to desired plants; or because they harbour particular insects or fungi. Ways of dealing with weeds without chemicals include growing smother crops, intercropping, removal before seed-set, hand weeding or mechanical disturbance, and mulching.

If you really must control a pest, choose a non-poisonous alternatives and use the least toxic control methods wherever possible, such as garlic spray.

Examples of mechanical methods include:

- ▶ spraying with a garden hose to blast insects off
- ▶ picking off insects
- ▶ removing or killing borers in tree trunks with wire protection (bands on trees, barriers to snails, milk cartons against cutworms)
- ▶ cut off affected parts and burn, otherwise responsibly remove them, such as placing them in an efficient compost system which will kill off disease organisms
- ▶ snail traps
- ▶ hand weeding
- ▶ heat or steam treatment of soil, rather than fumigation

COMPANION PLANTING

Companion planting is also useful. There are certain plants that mutually benefit the growth of each other and others that inhibit growth. For example cabbages grow well with onions and spinach but are incompatible with strawberries and tomatoes. Some aromatic plants deter some insects and others lure the predators of pests. For plants that deter insects try daisy pyrethrum, marigolds, basil, borage, sage, rosemary, thyme, nasturtium, dill and onions. Decide if total eradication is really necessary since reducing the problem or numbers may be enough. You only need to act when the problem arises, not just in case something may go wrong.

ABOVE: *Fennel repels aphids and spider mites.* **BELOW:** *Aromatic lavender wards off insects but attracts bees*

Companion flowers and what they do

- Alyssum   adds to organic level of soil
- Daisies   reduce nematodes
- Lupins   fix nitrogen into the soil
- Marigolds   reduce nematodes, reduce other pests, attracts hoverflies
- Petunias   repel insects
- Borage   attracts bees

Companion herbs and what they do

- Anise   deters aphids
- Basil   controls pests
- Borage   attracts bees, aids pollination
- Catnip   deters ants, aphids and others
- Chives   cures black spot on roses
- Dill   repels aphids and spider mites
- Eucalyptus   repels insects
- Garlic   good companion for fruit trees, repels vampires!
- Lemon balm   attracts bees, aids pollination
- Mustard   reduces aphids
- Rosemary   deters cabbage moth and other insects
- Sage   deters white cabbage moth
- Tansy   deters insects like ants, plant around fruit trees to repel fruit fly
- Wormwood   all round general insecticide, deters mice, slugs and snails

The seaweed solution

It is now known that brown kelp harvested from King Island is a wonderful regenerative tonic for plant strength and growth. When applied by spraying a seaweed solution over plant foliages it actually strengthens the cell walls of your plants making it tougher and able to resist insect damage and disease. It is very useful as a plant tonic for ailing plants, it encourages growth in vegetables and increases stem strength in seedlings. In fact many people have restricted garden maintenance to this one method.

HOMEMADE CONTROL TECHNIQUES

Homemade sprays have been used for centuries with variable results; the trick is to get in early so the insects are controlled before they reach plague proportions. Prevention is even better than cure. Try these recipes and ideas if you are considering limiting the chemicals used in your garden.

Leaf suckers and caterpillars

garlic spray recipe
- 6 cloves of garlic, crushed and chopped.
- A few rhubarb leaves for extra power.
- One cup of hot water. Leave to infuse overnight then strain and pour into a hand sprayer. Spray as needed to control caterpillars, aphids, snails, slugs, grasshoppers.

Caterpillars, leafhoppers and grasshoppers all love fresh, new, juicy leaves. If your plants are healthy you won't really notice the damage. A few chewed leaves won't matter much in the overall scheme of things but a plague needs action. Dipel is a safe bacterial spray that will not affect other beneficial insects.

Snails and slugs

These slimy creatures are really only a problem in wet weather. On wet evenings they quickly make light work of newly planted seedlings, young lettuces and baby tomatoes. They can eat a season's worth of salad in one night! Beer traps are effective and easy to make. Simply bury a jar filled with beer so the snails can slide straight into it. Stale beer will do (and snails aren't fussy about the brand either). The smell of hops will attract them from the entire garden. Snails dislike wood shavings, so try placing them as a barrier around your garden beds. A recent study has shown that used coffee grounds repel snails and slugs. Some proprietary baits contain poisonous substances and include a bittering agent to deter pets and children from ingesting the pellets.

CLOCKWISE FROM TOP LEFT:

▶ *Caterpillars delight in Busy Lizzie.*
▶ *Grasshoppers revel in soft rose buds.*
▶ *Snails and slugs go to town on hostas.*
▶ *Aphids love the new growth of roses.*
▶ *Black sooty mould on citrus.* ▶ *Sooty mould and hard white scale on pieris.* ▶ *White scale love michelis, gardenia and Madonna lily.*
▶ *Snails enjoy eating soft and tasty petals.*

The garden is a veritable zoological paradise of insects and disease. Try not to be too uptight with them as a balanced garden will always keep things in check, and there will be insects that will control other insects.

Multicrop has a product called Multiguard, which contains iron as the main snail and slug killer. Multiguard and Enviroguard are popular with gardeners because they aren't registered poisons. Personally I use the ancient, tried and tested technique of tread-on-'em, some strange people collect them and freeze them to death. Each to their own! Some gardeners swear by this recipe using garlic and soap, and if it doesn't end up deterring snails it may work well on vampires!

Aphids

Roses and citrus are particular favourites of aphids. You can either pull them off with a gloved hand or hose them off with a strong jet of water. Unfortunately these persistent critters breed quickly in huge numbers so you may need something stronger. Resort to Pyrethrum Long Life or garlic spray. Both are low-toxic sprays and do the job well. But don't forget that ladybeetle larvae are a natural control for aphids. Encourage the ladybirds into the garden. If you have many roses, find out about the aphid-eating predatory wasp from your rose supplier. Many parts of Australia already have predatory wasps in residence, as a result of recent release programs.

Mealy bug

Mealy bugs look like white flecks of cotton wool. They are the scourges of stressed, unloved and ignored indoor plants. Mealy bugs breed and multiply quickly, spreading to other plants. Control by isolating the affected plants and spraying with Confidor, which is a systemic, relatively low toxic spray. You can try dabbing them with methylated spirits on a cotton bud but be aware they have probably infiltrated the root system. Take the plant out of the pot and have a good poke around the roots. Always check newly purchased garden plants for this pest. For a non-chemical solution, wash plant roots and repot. Stressed gardenias in pots are very susceptible to root mealy bugs.

Scale insects

If left unchecked, scale can slowly suffocate roses, citrus, figs and many other garden treasures. Scale insects protect themselves with a waxy or hairy coating, so controlling them is difficult. The good news is that horticultural white oil and particularly PestOil will smother them and they can simply be brushed off. Repeat spray fortnightly up to eight times to control stubborn infestations. If you find serious scale hard to remove along the stems give them a good scrub with PestOil and an old toothbrush.

Sooty mould disease

When a plant is infested with scale, the insects secrete a sugary substance called honeydew. Sooty mould will grow on the honeydew, which compounds the problem. Sooty mould is a black fungus that looks as though the leaves have been sprinkled with charcoal soot. Aphids also secrete honeydew, so

> **snail spray recipe**
> • 6 cloves of crushed and chopped garlic
> • 2 tablespoons of mineral oil or liquid paraffin
> • ¹/2 litre of water
> • 1 tablespoon pure soap flakes
> Soak mixture overnight.
> To use dilute 3 teaspoons of the mixture to one litre of water. Spray as needed to control snails.

> **chive spray recipe**
> • 1 cup of chopped chives
> • 1 litre water
> Leave to infuse overnight then strain and pour into a sprayer. Spray as needed to control caterpillars, aphids, snails, slugs, and grasshoppers.

> **soapy water**
> ¹/2 cup of pure soap flakes. Agitate in 1 litre of water and spray. Deters black aphids on citrus and sooty mould on gardenias.

sooty mould can again be a secondary problem. Douse the leaves with soapy water (see inset) and hose off when dry, or spray and scrub with PestOil.

Curl grub

These guys do damage to seedlings and grass roots. There is no chemical cure, so as you find them in the soil feed them to the chooks or the birds.

milk spray recipe

- 1 part full cream milk to
- 9 parts water.

The fat in the milk acts as a protective coating to the leaves. Can be used to control fungal diseases on roses, grapes, cucumbers and begonias.

Powdery mildew/ downy mildew

These mildews are fungal problems that often occur on the leaves of zucchini, geranium, begonia, and sometimes fuchsia. They spread by spores and look like leaf discolouration. Caused by wet soils, poor drainage and wet foliage, it is wise to prevent this by watering the roots and not the leaves of susceptible plants. Control with a general fungicide like Mancozeb Plus or by applying wettable sulphur. Alternatively a milk spray (see inset), a development from Adelaide University.

Rose black spot

Control fungal diseases, such as black spot, by removing all affected leaves and placing them in the garbage bin. Do not add them to the compost. Spray all foliage with black spot rose spray or milk spray.

black spot rose spray

(developed by the Rose Society of America)
- 3 teaspoons of baking soda
- 3 tablespoons of PestOil
- 4 litres of water

Possum damage

Possums can do plenty of damage particularly to the fat ripe rose buds ready to burst into flower. A few methods have been tested with a variety of luck. Chilli sprays are often quite effective as is the product Deter.

chilli spray recipe

- 6 hot red chillis roughly chopped
- 1 litre of water

Infuse over night and spray over the rose buds that are in the path of pesky possums.

LEFT TO RIGHT: *Curl grub are a delicacy for birds. Powdery mildew attack zucchini. Black spot on roses. Possum damage can be cataclysmic. Try to impede their journey through your garden. Stop up all entrances into the roof and cap fences.*

inspire

mediterranean

It's a love affair that began in the distant hills overlooking Florence. A landscape of olive groves, enchanting villas and cypress. Filled with ancient stories. They say each cypress takes a soul to heaven.

The Mediterranean garden has become one of the most copied styles of the twenty-first century. Originally stemming from countries around the Mediterranean, this popular style combines the influence of such countries as Greece, France and Italy, and in particular regions of Santorini, Provence and Tuscany. The Mediterranean gardening approach relies on a sun-bleached feel with evocative plantings and romantic muted tones. Mediterranean gardens use drought-tolerant plants and a restricted colour palette within a simple design.

Through the long hot days of summer, flowers throw their shadows onto stark walls. Rough-textured dry-stone walls, sandstone paving and handmade bricks are chosen for warmth.

a mediterranean courtyard

GARDEN DESIGN PLAN

Space has become a luxury and small gardens force us to be creative. This means using plants imaginatively and making spaces multifunctional. This simple courtyard design creates an area in which to entertain, play and look at. The Tuscan terrace is the perfect platform to stage long alfresco Italian lunches. Formal planters and paving give an overall structure, while perennials and flowering shrubs add a lighter touch. Handmade pavers personalise the terrace and add charm. Garden beds wrap around, enclosing the space for privacy. Lawn, prone to drying out in summer, is kept to a minimum.

PLANTING KEY

1. Olive tree
2. Juniper 'Spartan'
3. Espalier orange
4. Lavender
5. Echeveria
6. Geraniums in planter boxes
7. Lawn

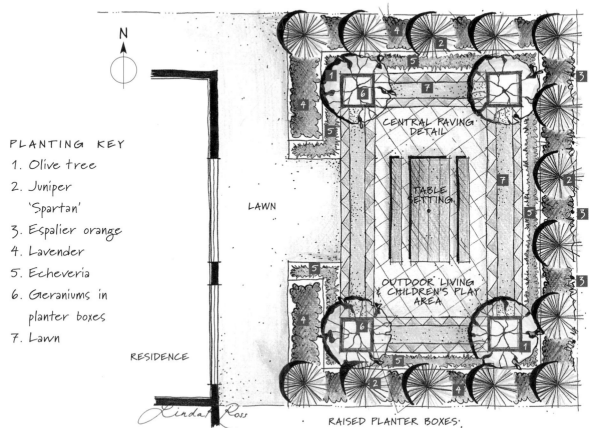

N

CENTRAL PAVING DETAIL

TABLE SETTING

OUTDOOR LIVING & CHILDREN'S PLAY AREA

LAWN

RESIDENCE

Linda Ross

RAISED PLANTER BOXES

OPPOSITE: *Mediterranean gardening makes particular sense in Australia. Simple splashes of colour bleached by the strong Australian sun, courtyards cooled with running water. Distinct plantings of gnarled olive trees, lavender, echium and cypress combine to create an evocative Tuscan atmosphere.* **ABOVE:** *Olives and grapes improve with age. Plant grapes for your children and olives for your children's children.*

SUITABLE CLIMATES

Arid zones, hot dry central Australia, Western Australia, central New South Wales, central Victoria and all of South Australia.

DESIGN TRICKS

By combining two functions into one area you can create a larger multifunctional space that can be used for a number of different activities. In this design we have combined the entertaining space with the children's play area.

By building four raised planters to seat level we have increased the areas in which to sit — negating the need for more furniture and clutter. This is a top tip in small spaces.

By painting the surrounding fence in a light colour we have immediately made the small courtyard seem larger.

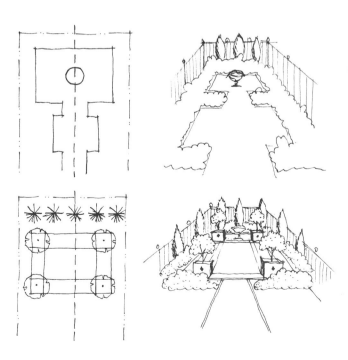

PLANTING SCHEME

Balance and proportion is important in this design. Mediterranean plants are robust and luxurious. The cypress trees grow up through the lavender, accentuating the landscape with their elegant tall green spires. Perfumed plants are included wherever possible. Formal clipped plantings contrast with the rampant nature of herbs, lavender, geraniums and pride of Madeira. Square planter boxes punctuate the corners of the garden. Each is planted with an olive tree and filled to the brim with bright red cascading geraniums. The olive is a symbol of peace, love, happiness and longevity. Each planter is bagged with ochre-coloured cement. A hedge of lavender surrounds the entertaining area, enveloping the courtyard with its sweet perfume.

Use the hot western facing walls to espalier citrus — a very effective space saving device. Train the branches horizontally along wires attached to the fence and you will be harvesting in the first year. Plant lemons, limes, oranges and red grapefuit.

Cool the courtyard with a western positioned pergola, and use this opportunity to grow your own grapes. Grapes need cool winters and low summer humidity, or mildew will become a problem. Birds can be a nuisance, so cover vines with netting or simply place paper bags over each grape cluster.

planting list

▶ Agapanthus hybrids
▶ Assorted herbs
▶ Blue chalksticks (*Senecio serpens*)
▶ Bougainvillea
▶ Cotton lavender (*Santolina chamaecyparissus*)
▶ Edible figs
▶ Grape vine (*Vitis vinifera*)
▶ Lavender (*Lavendula* hybrids)
▶ Myrtle (*Luma apiculata*)
▶ Oleander (*Nerium oleander*)
▶ Olive (*Olea europaea var. europaea*)
▶ Oranges and lemons (*Citrus* sp.)
▶ Pelargoniums
▶ Pride of Madeira (*Echium candicans*)
▶ Spartan junipers (*Juniperus* 'Spartan')
▶ Succulents (*Echeveria, Sedum, Cotyledon*)

LEFT: *Tuscan colours: shining silver foliage of olives and the mauve carpet of lavender make perfect companions.*

Pelargoniums

Lavender

Grapes

Pelargoniums

Blue chalksticks

plant profiles

 height & width of plant

 good for pot

 prefers full sun

 prefers partial shade

 tolerates full shade

 frost hardy

 frost tender

LEFT: *Oranges.* **RIGHT:** *Olives fruit after several years.*

ORANGE
Citrus sinensis

    4 m x 3 m

good for large tubs

Want fresh oranges and lemons but have no room to plant a tree? When space is at a premium, use your vertical space and espalier citrus onto a western-facing wall. Here they will drink in the sunshine and soon provide you with great fruit throughout the year. Try espaliering oranges, lemons or maybe a lime — they are each reminiscent of Italy and will provide a terrific artistic feature. Gradually stretch the lateral stems and fix to the fence. Prune lateral branches that won't fit the desired shape. The horizontal stems will produce fruit along the length of the bough.

Pick off all fruit for the first three years and then allow only a few to mature. Citrus are gross feeders, so fertilise with specialised citrus food three times a year, in spring, autumn and winter.

OLIVE
Olea europaea subsp. europaea

   4 m x 2 m

good for tubs

Olives are long-lived trees that are known for their distinctive silvery-grey canopy and knotted charcoal trunks. Fruits develop after several years, in summer and can be pickled green or black. If you dislike the fruit dropping and creating a mess, look out for a new non-fruiting variety. In Italy they say you plant grapes for your children and olives for your grandchildren. Your patience will be eventually rewarded.. Don't mistake it for the African olive, which can quickly become a weed. Olives enjoy well-drained soils and full sun. Feed with fruit-tree fertiliser and cow manure in early sping.

FROM LEFT TO RIGHT: *Juniperus 'Spartan'. Old terracotta pots filled with pelargoniums. Sweet smelling lavender.*

SPARTAN JUNIPER
Juniperus chinensis 'Spartan'

   2 m x 0.5 m

green foliage makes a good background

Use spartan junipers instead of the true Italian cypress as they are more garden friendly. Spartan junipers are the perfect size making them ideal garden specimens. They will grow into a handsome natural spire if left unclipped.

> Mulch Spartan junipers well and add manure-enriched compost.

IVY GERANIUMS
Pelargonium Ivy-leafed hybrids

    0.4 m x 0.4 m

long flowering period

What other flowering plant can provide so much intense colour throughout the warmer months? Choose one colour of geranium to give you a simple and stylish display. Treat ivy geraniums just like annuals, replacing them every third year by propagating cuttings. This way they will continue to look healthy and remain fungus free. Choose 'Laced Red Cascade' for its intense red floral display that is reminiscent of the Riviera.

> Keep ivy geraniums on the dry side. Trim frequently to encourage new flushes and to keep compact. Feed with Thrive for Flowering Plants or Garden Gold.

LAVENDER
Lavendula angustifolia

    1 m x 1 m

indigo flower spires

There are thousands of lavenders available, mostly originating from the Mediterranean region. Long flower heads of purple spires and their heavenly fragrance give a feast for the senses. Mass plant for best effect. Most will continue to flower throughout winter.

> Give lavender a haircut when it finishes flowering at the end of winter. Lavenders will not tolerate wet feet, so keep the garden bed on the dry side and mound the soil to improve drainage.

make your own paving border

Use paving borders to accentuate different areas and to reinforce the ground pattern.
• Mark a line on the ground for the border.
• Cut your square pavers diagonally with a brick saw to make two triangles.
• Measure the height of one triangle.
• Dig out a trench the width of the height of the triangle to a depth of 150 mm. Allow the soil walls to act as formwork
• Fill with concrete.
This will be the footing for your pavers.
• Place the triangle pavers along one side.
Use a stringline to make sure they are straight. Tap in place with a rubber mallet.
• On the opposite side press pebbles, tiles or marbles straight into the wet concrete to create a colourful pattern.
• Leave to cure for 24 hours.

garden features

PAVING DESIGN

When space is limited make the most out of multi-functional areas. The outdoor area in this design can double as another entertaining room. The paving design is based on a diagonal pattern within a formal border. We chose a sandy, ochre-coloured paver (400 mm x 400 mm), which fits in with the bleached Mediterranean style. A border of alternating colours (ochre and soft terracotta) defines the entertaining space and accentuates the formal design.

The secret to good paving is in the preparation. To ensure your paving area won't sink or buckle, compact each bedding layer of aggregate and paving sand. Avoid pooling water by laying the pavers on a slight gradient — the gradient needs to be only one or two per cent. Set these levels by using string lines. First lay the 50-mm aggregate bedding layer and compact with a plate compactor. Add a 50-mm layer of paving sand and compact again. Lay the pavers carefully — using a string line to keep the paving level and maintain 5-mm gaps between each paver. Sweep paving sand into these 5-mm gaps to finish. Securing the paving edge with a concrete strip will add strength and stop movement.

PAVERS

There are as many different materials used for paving as there are paving styles. Materials range from brick, terracotta, reconstituted stone, sand-stone, bluestone — the list is endless. Choose a material that is within your budget and is in keeping with the style of your home. If you are worried about constructing a paved area yourself, seek the expertise of a professional paver or landscaper. Obtain several quotes and if possible check out their previous jobs in your area. For a recommendation try the Landscape Contractors Association.

GARDEN CARE

Cumquats, oranges, lemons, limes and grapefruit are easy to grow and provide us with extraordinary quantities of vitamin C. Citrus trees need plenty of room, so don't crowd them with other plants. They also need lots of sunlight. Overshadowing will cause reduced fruit yields. Mulch around the tree but keep the mulch slightly away from the trunk to prevent collar rot. Make sure your citrus don't dry out in the summer. Let the fruit sweeten and ripen on the tree while providing frequent deep watering. Give them three feeds of a specialised citrus food a year in spring, autumn and winter. If you are having a problem with pollination, plant borage underneath the citrus to encourage bees. Treat citrus leaf miner with a regular spraying of PestOil, which coats the leaf to deter the bug. Keep bronze citrus bug away with Confidor, or simply vacuum them off. (Don't laugh, many gardeners use this method.)

Succulents grow best with a little attention. Water and feed in the growing spring season. Trim off finished flowers and lanky stems.

Lavenders are quick to become leggy and dry. To

ABOVE: *Deep irrigate citrus well in summer to reduce the risk of fruit drop.*

prevent this, lightly prune after flowering, and replace the plant after every five to seven years. You can simply replace by taking cuttings from the original plant.

Junipers and olives can remain unpruned as they will develop their distinctive shape on their own. Mulch well and watch them grow.

the potted Mediterranean garden
Add elements such as climbers, succulents and annuals in pots to soften the formality of the design. Fill pots with colourful seasonal plants, such as agapanthus, lavender, geraniums, oleander and succulents. Italian water jars and assorted terracotta pots placed on their sides, upturned or broken add a touch of Tuscany. Nurseries are often willing to offload broken pots for next to nothing. A feature succulent (*Echeveria* 'Violet Queen') gently spills over a classical urn and is the focal point of our courtyard. Other recommendations include any of the echeverias, sedums, sempervivems or crassulas. These are all sun-hardy plants that will survive without any work.

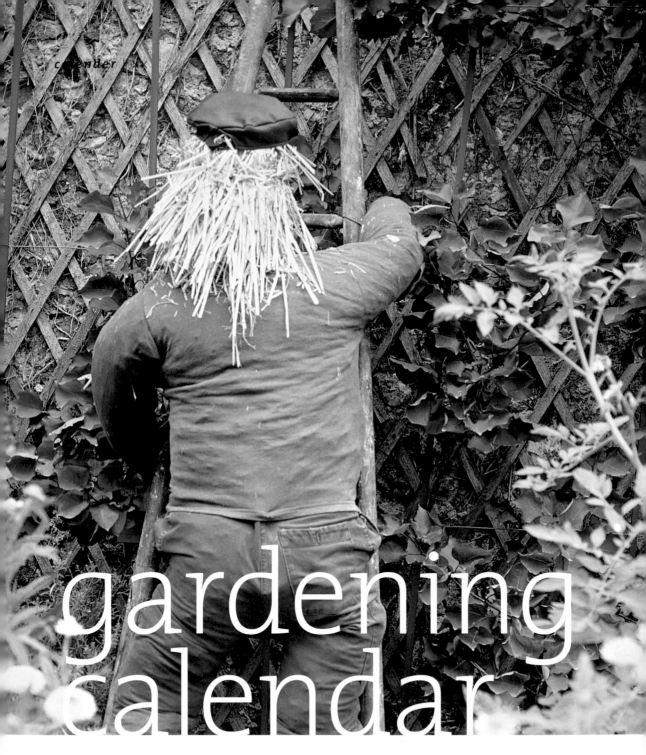

gardening calendar

For everything there is a season and a certain time for every task. But when on earth is the correct time? Here is your guide of what to do and when.

spring

Spring is the season of renewal. The daylight hours lengthen, the soil gradually warms up and the sap flows through the plants more quickly. Deciduous plants dress their bare branches with delicate veils of bright green foliage. Bees, birds and insects are all busy as life is replenished in the spring garden.

THINGS TO DO

Feed the entire garden with organic matter or compost. Spread about 5 cm of compost over all your beds and water in well. The compost will gradually work its way into the soil with the help of the earthworms. Use well-rotted cow, horse or chicken manure, and vermi-compost (worm waste) from your worm farm.

ANNUALS

Spring flowering pansies and primulas will complement daffodils, tulips and all the spring-flowering bulbs. Keep your new annuals healthy by adding seaweed liquid to the watering can. Tip-prune the young annuals to encourage bushy growth and regularly deadhead finished flowers. Feed with Thrive for Flowers to prolong flowering. Plant out annuals, such as petunias, for your Christmas display.

BULBS AND PERENNIALS

After flowering, feed bulbs with a liquid fertiliser and allow the leaves to die down naturally. Lift hyacinths and tulips when the foliage has browned completely and store in a paper

ABOVE: *Jonquils herald spring and emerge better each year.*

bag in a cool dry spot. Most bulbs, such as daffodils, bluebells, freesias, sparaxis and jonquils, can be left *in situ* to grow and divide.

ROSES

Roses need plenty of cow manure in spring, a mulch of lucerne hay and a good dose of rose food. Look after water shoots that come from above the graft. They will carry the healthiest growth. Shoots below the graft are suckers and can be removed. Keep an eye out for aphids. Hose them off, wipe them off or spray them with soapy water (see page 130). Confidor is the safest chemical to spray, as it doesn't enter the food chain.

SHRUBS AND TREES

Spray azaleas and rhododendrons with Bayleton from the time the buds start to colour and remove all flowers affected by petal blight. After flowering, prune lightly then protect new growth from lace bug attack with Confidor, or you may prefer to use PestOil as an alternative. Spray the undersurface of the leaves every fortnight to prevent attack. Mulch azaleas with well-rotted cow manure and water well with seaweed extract to strengthen them.

Mulch gardenias with compost, water well and feed them with a controlled release fertiliser to promote flowering in summer. Dose them with Epsom salts or iron/magnesium chelates if the leaves are yellowing. Watch out for scale and sooty mould, and treat either problem with PestOil.

ABOVE: *Crank up the kitchen garden now to reap rewards in summer.* **BELOW:** *Cymbidium orchids should be repotted after flowering.*

VEGETABLES

Plant herbs and vegetables after the threat of frost has passed. Remember to stagger the planting of vegetables so they don't all ripen at once. Try tomatoes, basil, coriander, parsley, Spanish onion, silverbeet, rocket, beetroot, lettuce, spring onion, corn, pumpkin or melons. Regularly feed with Powerfeed, Harvest, composted cow manure or liquid seaweed. Keep well watered. Two easy crops the kids will love are seed potatoes and a mushroom farm.

LAWNS

Replant or renovate tired lawn areas. Top-dress bare patches, and if your lawn is hard and compacted use a garden fork to open up the soil to allow more oxygen and water to reach the roots of the grass. Liquid feed with a seaweed solution and an organic soluable feed.

CITRUS

Every season is a good season to feed citrus except in the heat of summer. Use pelleted manure, your own compost or a specialised citrus food. Prune out any diseased or straggly branches. Watch out for the young bronze orange stink bugs. Begin a fortnightly spraying regime with PestOil to prevent citrus leaf minor, sooty mould and scale.

POTTED GARDEN

Early spring is a good time to repot container plants. Repot them into a larger pot or trim the roots slightly and repot into the same size pot. New potting mix will supply essential nutrients for spring growth. Add a granular fertiliser and water retention crystals to the potting mix, then top up the pots with compost or manure. Divide orchids and repot after flowering using a special orchid bark, and then position in a shadier spot for summer.

PRUNING

Don't prune frost-damaged plants until after the last frost so as to help protect the other parts of the plant. Prune spring-flowering shrubs,

tool talk
Keep your pruning tools sharp and clean. This way you won't spread disease and you'll make a clean cut.

ornamental fruit trees after the flowers fade, banksia roses, weigelas, maybushes, azaleas, rhododendrons, viburnums, abelias and ornamental flowering peaches. Australian plants need attention too. Keep grevillea, bottlebrush, correa and banksia lightly pruned after flowering to encourage compact growth and another flush of flowers.

summer

Scorching sun, drying winds and long hours of intense heat are enough to make even the most committed gardener bolt for the coast and the open seas! But don't despair, you can do things to bring relief to your poor scorched garden.

THINGS TO DO

Most importantly, spread a 10-cm layer of mulch on your garden beds to reduce water evaporating from the bare soil. Mulching will also prevent weed growth and keep the roots of your plants cool. Practise water-wise gardening to keep the water bill down and to maintain healthy plants during the hot dry spells (see page 118).

ANNUALS

When the warmth of summer arrives continue to feed annuals with a liquid fertiliser such as Thrive for Flowering Plants to prolong flowering. Regularly remove old blooms and wayward growth. Plant seedlings late in the day, when conditions are cooler, and protect tender plants from hot winds. Dunk new plants in their pots and seedlings in their punnets in a weak solution of seaweed before planting to ensure that the roots are thoroughly moist. Spray seedlings with a fine mist to lower moisture loss. Annuals suitable for temperate zones include ageratum, aster, gypsophila, pansy, petunia, phlox, sweet William, verbena and zinnias. In subtropical to tropical zones choose chrysanthemum, cleome, gazania, geranium, gerbera, nasturtium, petunia and salvia.

BULBS AND PERENNIALS

Summer is a good season to order bulbs and perennials from nursery catalogues to plant in autumn. The earlier you order, the more likely your selections will be available for delivery and planting in autumn. Look at our list of great mail order nurseries across Australia on page 152.

Agapanthus are guaranteed to bloom spectacularly in summer with little maintenance. Grow them near a pool to pick up the vibrant blue water, use them to bind soil on a sloping bank or to grace a sweeping driveway. Pop dwarf agapanthus into a small space or a pot and enjoy their profusion of flowers. Look for dwarf white 'Snowstorm', 'Baby Blue' and 'Tinkerbell', which has variegated foliage. A deep purple agapanthus, 'Purple Cloud', has caught my eye, and 'Wavy Navy' offers huge blooms on 1.5 metre long stems. Plant agapanthus in enriched soil, as you will not move them for years, and give them a drink in hot weather and a dressing of pelleted manure after flowering.

ROSES

Lightly prune shrub roses to encourage the next flush of flowers. Do this by continually picking blooms on long stems for floral arrangements. Feed with a rose fertiliser such as Organic Life for a fabulous autumn display. Water well and mulch with lucerne hay. Summer humidity encourages fungal diseases, such as black spot and powdery mildew. Deep watering every three to four weeks with a watering can of seaweed solution will help roses resist such diseases. Control

ABOVE: *Simple. The more roses you pick the more roses you will get.*

fungal diseases, such as black spot, by removing affected leaves and putting them in the garbage bin, not the compost. Spray fortnightly all foliage with Black Spot Rose Spray or Milk Spray (see page 131).

SHRUBS AND TREES

Hydrangeas have the most glorious summer flowers that cool the hottest garden. They thrive in moist soil enriched with plenty of compost. They prefer filtered shade and protection from hot sun and summer winds that will quickly scorch their gorgeous flowers. In summer, an evening drink will miraculously revive them. Water regularly with a long, deep drink, and ensure they are mulched. Cut flowers in the early morning, crush the stems and soak them to their necks in water for an hour or so.

VEGETABLES

In temperate zones plant out beans, beetroot, lettuce, radish, silverbeet, tomato, snow peas, spring onions and rocket. In tropical areas, plant lettuce, pumpkin, radish, silverbeet, broccoli and spring onions. Late planting of beans and tomatoes will lengthen your harvest into early winter. If growing vegetables in containers, select dwarf-growing varieties that take up less room but give good yields.

> Growing your own onions is great, but it is hard to know when they are ready to harvest. For best results plant them on the shortest day of the year and harvest them on the longest day.

LAWNS

Don't mow your lawn too short in summer otherwise it will scorch. Instead, apply Yates Lawn Tamer to slow down the growth. Remove clumps of paspalum, summer grass, dandelion and Paterson's curse by removing just below ground level with a sharp knife or hoe. Stop the cycle by getting them before they go to seed.

CITRUS

Keep up the deep watering and check for leaf curl miner and stink bugs. The water they get now will have direct results on the size of your fruit, juiciness and fruit drop. Make sure your citrus are mulched well. Resist feeding citrus now, as it is too hot.

POTTED GARDEN

This is the harshest month for potted plants as they dry out in a day. Put a saucer under each pot to conserve water. When going away on holidays put all your potted plants on the cooler southern side of the house and cover with shadecloth. Give them a big drink before leaving and ask a friend to check on them. Mist indoor plants regularly to increase humidity and deter pests. Wipe leaves with a cloth soaked in half water and half milk to keep them dust-free. A preventative spray of PestOil will also keep leaves healthy and free of disease. Feed with a controlled release fertiliser every three months.

PRUNING

Take control of wisteria and other vigorous vines now. Trim leggy, young shoots to keep the plants bushy and neat. Cut bougainvillea back hard to the main branches to keep it contained and maximise the colour next year. Prune spring-flowering shrubs to improve their shape and remove dead flowers. This includes spiraea (maybush), deutzia and ceanothus. Prune summer flowers after flowering, such as impatiens, hibiscus, gardenia, murraya and plumbago. Prune stone fruit trees — plum, peach and apricot — after you pick the year's crop.

Temperatures in excess of 40°C will cause foliage to scorch. Do not prune the scorched foliage until you are quite sure that the threat of scorching is over, otherwise fragile growth in the interior of the plant will be the first to go and the plant will find it hard to recuperate twice.

> *waterwise*
> Once your garden is established, install a watering system to make watering the garden next summer much easier and more efficient. A drip micro-irrigation system attached to a timer is essential insurance for the busy gardener.

autumn

Make the most of the mild days before rugging up and moving indoors. As the shadows lengthen and evenings cool, it's a refreshing change from summer. Lie on a blanket and watch the leaves change colour and fall from the trees. Gather warmth around you and stock up the woodpile.

THINGS TO DO

In temperate climates autumn is the best season to plant. In cold climates it is better to wait until spring as plants will have the time to make essential root growth while the soil is still warm. As the temperatures drop, plants will become dormant, ready for huge foliage growth in spring. It's a good idea to prepare the planting hole well ahead of planting time, adding compost to a hole as big as you can manage. Now purchase your plants and get them in the ground as soon as possible.

ANNUALS

You are spoilt for choice with autumn flowers. In sunny spots, plant iceland poppy, cornflower, snapdragon, stock and nemesia. Cineraria, lobelia and primula are good for shadier garden areas; plant them in a carpet beneath bare magnolias and other deciduous trees. Sweet peas are an old-fashioned favourite. Use them to disguise ugly fences. They are traditionally planted out on St Patrick's Day, 17 March, but don't despair if you miss it as they can be planted throughout autumn. Look out for the perfumed perennial sweet peas and grow them on tripods and up ladders for something different.

BULBS AND PERENNIALS

Plant your bulbs now for a brilliant and dazzling display. Label them as you plant them or plant them in bulb baskets so they can be easily located when they have died back. Alternatively, bulbs can be 'naturalised' in lawns beneath large trees — daffodil, bluebell and freesia are the best choice for this purpose. Remember not to mow this lawn until the bulbs have finished flowering and their leaves have died back.

Some of the most reliable bulbs are jonquil, snowflake, freesia, sparaxis, ixia, babiana, bluebell and daffodil. A drift of golden daffodils planted in autumn will flower in winter and herald the approach of spring. If you choose tulips or hyacinths, give them a pretend winter in the crisper of your fridge for six to eight weeks and then plant them in a sunny spot. If you only have limited space, grow your bulbs in shallow pots.

Most perennials flower through summer and autumn, especially if you regularly remove spent flower stems to

ABOVE: *A colourful explosion marks a change in temperature.*

prolong the flowering season. Perennial asters, day lilies, salvias and pokers all respond to summer pruning. Regular deep watering with seaweed solution will also help prolong flowering. A few summer perennials, such as foxgloves, shasta daisies, agapanthus, day lilies, and evening primrose can be lifted, divided and replanted later in autumn. Tidy up all perennials that have just finished flowering.

ROSES

May is a good time to plant roses in the garden. Select a position with plenty of sun, good drainage and lots of nutritious soil. An economical way to purchase roses is to buy bare-rooted plants ordered ahead of time from specialist rose nurseries or purchased from reputable garden centres. Prepare the planting hole by digging in cow manure, and carefully follow the directions so the roots are not damaged. The sooner they are in the ground the better.

Constantly hack back established hybrid tea and English roses to encourage further flushes of flowers throughout the autumn season ... the more you pick, the more flowers you'll get. Keep up the cow and pelleted manures and compost. Water roses on the ground to prevent fungal diseases. Mulch with lucern hay.

SHRUBS AND TREES

Autumn is the best time to select deciduous trees when they are in full autumn colour. Although the weather conditions may cause variation in colour intensity from year to year, some trees do colour better than others. Visit a good deciduous tree nursery while their autumn foliage is on show. The following deciduous trees have autumn colours and are suitable for a small garden, unlike the giant liquidambar:

Planting a tree *A tree needs a hole at least one metre square of well-conditioned soil so that its new roots can spread out into friendly territory to support its developing trunk and branches. A miserable hole means a miserable tree that will never reach its full potential. Position the stake before planting as it will damage roots if it's done later. Tie with a hessian band in a figure of eight. Make a saucer-like depression around your new tree so that any water or rain will soak in towards the trunk and not run off and be wasted. Always water your new trees and shrubs with one full watering can of seaweed solution. This will eliminate air pockets from the root zone and reduce planting shock for the roots.*

ABOVE: *Loved for its lime foliage,* **Robinia** *is a handsome tree. Best planted where there is minimal disturbance to the root zone as it is quick to sucker.*

- ▶ Chinese Fringe Tree (*Chinonanthus retusus*)
- ▶ Chinese Tallowwood (*Sapium sebiferum*)
- ▶ Crepe Myrtle (*Lagerstroemia indica* Indian Summer Range)
- ▶ Flowering Dogwood (*Cornus florida*)
- ▶ Japanese Maple (*Acer japonicum* 'Dissectum')
- ▶ Maidenhair Tree (*Gingko biloba*)
- ▶ Manchurian Pear (*Pyrus ussuriensis*)
- ▶ Ornamental Crabapple (*Malus floribunda* or *M. ioensis* 'Plena')
- ▶ Ornamental Pear (*Pyrus* 'Chanticleer', 'Aristocrat')
- ▶ Persimmon (*Parrotia persica*)
- ▶ Pompom Tree (*Dais cotinifolia*)
- ▶ Silk Floss tree (*Albizzia julibrissin*)

These trees are suitable for larger gardens:
- ▶ *Gleditsia* 'Ruby Lace'
- ▶ Lipstick Maples (*Acer* 'Autumn Glory')
- ▶ Pin Oak (*Quercus pinatus*)
- ▶ Poinciana (*Delonix reginea*)
- ▶ *Robinia pseudoacacia* 'Frisia'
- ▶ Tupelo (*Nyssa sylvatica*)
- ▶ White-trunked Himalayan Birch (*Betula* 'Jacquemontii')

winter As the days

shorten I'm ready to hibernate.
Take cover from cloudy skies, arm yourself
with unread garden books, mail order
catalogues and magazines. It's time to
quieten down and catch up.

VEGETABLES

When summer vegetables finish renew the soil and plant for winter. Vegetables that do well in cooler weather are lettuce, spinach, parsnip, beetroot, onions, leeks, and ruby chard. Plant peas and beans in a well-limed soil; don't forget sugar snap and snow peas for stir-fries. If space permits grow cabbage, cauliflower, broccoli and brussel sprouts. When space is at a premium plant smaller dwarf varieties of vegetables that produce just as much on smaller-sized plants. As summer herbs finish, plant parsley. Plant out the cloves from garlic and grow rosemary to flavour roasts.

LAWNS

Repair worn areas with lawn seed and feed grass before onset of the cooler weather. Fertilise with organic lawn feed and time this for when it's raining, this will help the nutrient to get down to the root zone. Top dress any dips and holes in the lawn.

CITRUS

Feed citrus with a specialised citrus food. Remove immature fruit from young citrus trees as they have not established their strong framework to carry such weight. Wait until the tree is around six years old before allowing it to bear fruit.

POTTED GARDEN

Bring cymbidium orchids out of their shady spots into a little more sun to promote flowering. Feed with specialised orchid food to encourage more flower spikes. Trim any old flower heads from potted succulents to keep them looking tidy.

PRUNING

Gently trim any scorched leaves left from summer early in the season. Hedges such as box, lilly pilly, murraya and lophomyrtus can be shaped now. Roses can be hacked back to encourage their autumn flush.

THINGS TO DO

This is the time to restructure and rethink your garden. Most plants will be dormant so now is the time to move them around and look at the overall design of the garden. Prepare new garden beds for spring annuals and perennials. No matter what soil you have, it will always benefit from additional organic matter. Use lucerne hay, chicken manure, mushroom compost, cow manure or compost. Make sure you add well-rotted manure, as fresh manure will burn plant roots. Clay-based soils could benefit from one or two applications of Clay Breaker (see page 114).

ANNUALS

Cinerarias and snowdrops grow beautifully under deciduous magnolias and contribute to a colourful wintry scene. Continue to fertilise winter and spring-flowering annuals with Thrive for Flowering Plants. Watering with seaweed solution will keep pansies, primula, poppies and cinerarias healthy and growing strongly. Pinch out growing tips to encourage bushiness and remove spent flower heads for a better flower display.

BULBS AND PERENNIALS

Summer-flowering perennials will cease flowering with the onset of the cooler weather. Now it's time to remove dead foliage and tidy clumps. Completely

149

renovate your perennials every three years. Dig them up and divide with a sharp spade. You may have some left over to give away to friends. Add liberal amounts of compost to your perennial garden and cultivate well. Plant perennials back into the reconditioned soil and water in with a seaweed solution. Some of my favourites include lilium, day lily, pokers, agapanthus hybrids, shasta daisies, perennial aster, sunflower, canna lily, dahlia, ornamental grass, salvia, eupatorium, anthemis, rudbeckia, helichrysum, wormwood, coneflower and yarrow. Plant out summer-flowering

ABOVE: *Magnolia x soulangiana will flower towards the end of winter ... a reminder that all is not lost.*

bulbs such as hippeastrum, lilium and dahlia tubers. Dahlias thrive on the east coast and there are some great ones to choose from, like the purple-foliaged, red-flowering 'Bishop of Llandarff'.

ROSES

Resist the temptation to prune roses until July or August, when the risk of frost has passed. Prune with sharp clean secateurs. Do not prune spring flowering roses until after they have bloomed. Winter is a great time to choose new roses from the bare-rooted selection available at nurseries and through mail order from specialist rose nurseries (see the Appendix on page 152).

SHRUBS AND TREES

Once your trees and shrubs are bare they will be dormant, which means the sap is not flowing and you can move them if you need to. Moving large trees is a big job and should only be undertaken if absolutely necessary. Spray evergreen plants all over with Stressguard to reduce transpiration rate and transplant shock.

In cold and temperate zones plant camellias to add massive splashes of autumn and winter colour. In shadier areas plant the large-flowering, large-leafed japonicas. Their enormous flowers are bold and colourful. In sunnier areas choose the small-leaved sasanquas, which will delight you with their full coverage of flowers. Camellias grow just about

bare branches, bare roots
Winter is an excellent time to plant deciduous shrubs and trees. These are generally long-lived additions so plan their position carefully. Make sure the soil has been improved beforehand. If you are planting bare-rooted plants, soak the clay seal off the root ball and then spread the roots carefully and evenly over a mound of improved soil in the planting hole.

ABOVE: *Rainbow chard or spinach can be grown throughout winter* **BELOW:** *Prune hydrangeas back to a pair of plump leaf buds.*

anywhere in neutral to acid, well-drained soils, and are famous for having no major problems. Trim sasanquas into shape as they finish flowering and encourage bushiness by tip-pruning lanky growth. They appreciate a thick mulch of manure.

In humid-temperate areas spray azaleas as soon as the buds begin to show some colour with a fungicide, such as Bayleton, to control petal blight. Azaleas struggle in tropical and subtropical zones, as they are prone to red spider mite, petal blight and lacebug.

VEGETABLES

The vegetable garden will remain productive through winter if there is enough sun. Peas, silverbeet, cabbage, broad beans and carrots are among the easiest to grow and can be planted throughout the winter months. Keep vegetables thriving with regular applications of liquid seaweed.

LAWNS

Check your lawn for poor drainage in prolonged wet periods. You may need to install a drain to prevent waterlogging and the resulting problems of dead grass. The curse of winter lawns is the wretched bindi-eye. Spray with BinDie or just dig them out. Improve the vigour of your lawn so it will choke out weeds. Winter grass is an annual weed that will set seed in spring and spread through the lawn. Treat with Yates Winter Grass Killer or Endothal from Garden King.

CITRUS

It is better to feed your citrus in midwinter than to feed them in the heat of summer. Check them for scale, especially hard scale that appears as white flecks on woody stems. Spray with PestOil to control soft scale, young bronze orange bugs and citrus leaf miner.

POTTED GARDEN

Indoor plants generally need less water in winter than in the warmer months but winter heating tends to dry out the indoor atmosphere, which can be very hard on plants. Maintain humidity by regular misting or placing a bowl of water in heated rooms. In colder climates it may be necessary to bring tropical potted plants indoors. Stop watering potted cacti and succulents altogether.

PRUNING

Cut back deciduous trees and shrubs in July. Hydrangeas can be pruned now by removing old woody stems at the base to provide room for new growth. Cut remaining stems to a plump pair of leaf buds. Apply lime for pink flowers or Hydrangea Bluing for blue flowers. Do not prune spring-flowering shrubs, such as azalea, weigela, viburnum, ceonothus, deutzia, philadelphus, maybush and ornamental flowering blossom trees, as you'll prune the bud wood, leave pruning until after flowering.

appendix

Your guide to my favourite plant growers, and the tools you will need to get your garden growing.

mail order nurseries

The Blue Dandenongs Bulb Farm
(03) 9751 9555
www.blued.com.au

Bulb Express
1800 677 437
www.bulbexpress.com.au

Bulbs Direct
(03) 5272 2066
www.bulbsdirect.com.au

Daley's Fruit Tree Nursery
www.daleysfruit.com.au

Diggers Seeds
www.diggers.com.au

Eastcoast Perennials
P.O. Box 323, Wauchope 2446

Fulham Grange (bulbs)
1800 677 824
www.fulhamgrange.com.au

Lambley Nursery (perennials)
(03) 53434303

Mistydowns (roses and perennials)
(03) 5345 6575
www.mistydowns.com.au

Montburg Gardens
(03) 5265 1198
www.montburggardens.com.au

Mountain View Daylily Nursery
(07) 5494 2346
www.daylily.com.au

Orchid Oasis Orchid Nursery
(02) 6553 2991
email: oasisorc@pnc.com.au

Paradise Distributors
(07) 5441 5921
email: araplants@iprimus.com.au

Ross Roses
(08) 8556 2555
www.rossroses.com.au

Sydney Wildflower Nursery West
(02) 9628 4448
www.nativenursery.com.au/SWNWest

Swanes Nurseries (roses)
(02) 9651 1322
www.swanes.com.au

Tesselaar Bulbs & Flowers
(03) 9737 9811
www.tesselaar.net.au

www.nurseriesonline.com.au
and check out classifieds in gardening magazines.

books

Gardening by Mail
Edited by Joan Richardson
Sally Milner Publishing
Distributed by Gary Allen Pty Ltd
(02) 9725 2933

The Aussie Plant Finder,
by Margaret Hibbert.
Published by Florilegium
(02) 9555 8589

gardening equipment

Make gardening as easy and as safe as possible by choosing the right tool for the right job. Gardening should always be a pleasure and working in the garden with the wrong tools quickly becomes frustrating and time consuming. Buy quality tools with good warranties rather than cheap tools for cheap prices. Good tools will last a lifetime.

GARDEN SPADE AND FORK

Digging involves both digging and lifting, so buy a good-quality garden spade and fork. There are ergonomic styles available for those of us with back problems. As for any good utensil, make sure the handle continues down into the head.

WHEELBARROW

A lightweight wheelbarrow is a handy way of moving soil and mulch. Keep it in the shed to prevent it from rusting.

MUCK RAKE

A muck rake quickly distributes mulch around the garden. Its lightweight handle and well-designed prongs make light work of an arduous task. It can also be used to collect animal manures from the paddock or cleaning out the compost bin.

PRUNERS

Good quality secateurs will last a lifetime. The blades can be replaced or resharpened, usually at your local nursery. Gardeners become very possessive of their secateurs. I know of two gardeners who keep a pair handy in their cars! Use secateurs to cut small diameter stems only, such as roses. Larger branches should be pruned with loppers or a pruning saw. Tip prune plants, like vegetables, with your fingers.

LAWN MOWER

I love a good push mower; I expect I'm a hippy at heart. Push mowers are great for small lawns and even better as I found recently when the petrol mower breaks down. Petrol mowers are often heavy and can be hard to move around if your garden is on different levels. Be wary of mowing over the cord when using electric mowers.

HEDGE TRIMMER

A light hedge or line trimmer will take the hard work out of hedge maintenance. A good stringline is also a helpful tool for this task.

FROM LEFT: *I find my muck rake invaluable for collecting leaves, mulching and composting. A good quality spade is essential when digging a good hole for Tree Day. This is all you need for a productive day in the garden.*

RAKE

A large wide-tooth rake quickly collects fallen leaves and bark and easily redistributes mulch.

MULCHER

Mulchers make light work of twigs and branches. You can put the mulch straight onto the garden or, as we do, straight onto the compost heap.

garden safety

There are plenty of dangers in the garden. They are wide, varied and sometimes lethal, so listen and learn for ways to keep safe. Potting mixes contain pathogens. Fertilisers, insecticides and fungicides are made up of potentially harmful chemicals. Garden tools can have a nasty bite. So take care and keep these simple safety rules in mind.

THE DOS AND DON'TS OF GARDEN SAFETY

- Bend at the knees to avoid straining your back.
- Use a kneepad when bending down to weed.
- If poisoning occurs, phone 131126 immediately. This is a 24-hour hotline.
- Wear steel-capped boots when mowing.

- Wear gloves, a hat and sunscreen when working in the garden.
- Wear safety goggles and earmuffs when using loud machinery, such as chainsaws, mulchers and whipper snippers.
- Take care not to inhale when opening a bag of soil and use soil marked with Australian standards.
- Keep all garden chemicals out of the reach of children, locked away in the garden shed.
- Clearly label all chemicals with an indelible marker.
- Always use the same container to mix weedkillers and mark as dangerous.
- Be aware of and able to identify all dangerous spiders and snakes living in your area. There are posters available for children and adults that show the differences.

POTTING MIXES

The main problem with potting mixes is their potential to carry Legionella bacteria. Legionella can live in potting mixes for up to one year even after being sterilised. If you suspect you have been infected, seek medical treatment straight away. Reduce your chance of infection by taking care not to inhale while opening a bag of soil or by wearing a mask. Keep your distance from the soil mix and wear gloves. When tipping soil out from the bag, try not to create too much dust.

TAKE CARE WITH GARDEN MACHINERY

Store garden tools and machinery in a locked shed. Mowers, chainsaws and pruning tools all have a hard bite. Wear protective clothing at all times — chaps, steel-capped boots, eye protection, gloves and earmuffs. Only use a chainsaw if you are experienced. There are short courses at TAFE on the safe use of chainsaws. Take care when mowing the lawn. Wear steel-capped boots to protect your feet.

LEFT: *Slip slop slap. Protect your skin with a hat and sunscreen every time you go into the garden.*

GARDEN CHEMICALS

Over the last century the garden industry has seen its fair share of dangerous chemicals. It's a wonder that some were used for so long. Most of the worst ones have now been banned. The main types of chemicals are organochlorines, carbamates, heavy metals, synthetic insecticides, mineral oils, herbicides, solvents and wetting agents.

What are the environmental effects?

Chemicals may affect organisms other than the pest they are intended for — it is estimated that as little as one per cent hit the target organism. Most chemicals are toxic not only to one particular organism but to others as well. Some chemicals are toxic to fish and other aquatic animals, bees, earthworms, birds and other beneficial wildlife. In addition, some chemicals are persistent so they continue to kill other organisms in the future.

Then there are the added difficulties of bio-accumulation (the chemical is stored in the body and levels build up) and biomagnification (increased concentration in animals higher up the food chain). Moreover, pests can develop a resistance to certain chemicals which causes the use of more toxic chemicals. Not a good idea! Some chemicals (such as Maneb and Zineb) break down to a product that is more toxic than the original chemical. All in all, it's safer to go chemical free.

Take precautions

There are plenty of alternatives to using chemicals but if you feel you have to spray with them there are a few safety precautions that must be followed.

▸ Always wear protective clothing and face mask.
▸ Don't spray around children or pets.

▸ Don't spray on a windy day.
▸ Make sure there is no overspray.
▸ Follow the instructions on the label regarding its strength and application.

ABOVE: *Safely store garden chemicals on the top shelf of the garden shed and keep it locked.*

The way in which to store chemicals is also important. Padlock or key lock any central storage area and keep the key hidden from tiny fingers. Always store hazardous chemicals out of reach of children.

safety first Never store chemicals in soft drink bottles or anything that looks like it could be good to drink. Clearly label the contents and date on all containers with an indelible marker so as not to forget what's in there. Phone the national **Poison's Information line** immediately on **131126** in an emergency with chemicals. The number is manned 24 hours a day. Each poison has its own individual treatment according to its major ingredients.

index

general index

158